Demystifying
MTSS

A School and District Framework
for Meeting Students' Academic and
Social-Emotional Needs

Matt Navo   Amy Williams

Solution Tree | Press

a division of
Solution Tree

555 North Morton Street
Bloomington, IN 47404
800.733.6786 (toll free) / 812.336.7700
FAX: 812.336.7790

email: info@SolutionTree.com
SolutionTree.com

Visit **go.SolutionTree.com/schoolimprovement** to download the free reproducibles in this book.

Printed in the United States of America

Library of Congress Cataloging-in-Publication Data

Names: Navo, Matt, author. | Williams, Amy, author.
Title: Demystifying MTSS : a school and district framework for meeting
   students' academic and social-emotional needs / Matt Navo, Amy Williams.

Description: Bloomington, IN : Solution Tree Press, 2022. | Includes
   bibliographical references and index.
Identifiers: LCCN 2021061008 (print) | LCCN 2021061009 (ebook) | ISBN
   9781951075699 (paperback) | ISBN 9781951075705 (ebook)
Subjects: LCSH: Multi-tiered systems of support (Education) | Professional
   learning communities. | Social learning--Study and teaching. | Emotional
   intelligence.
Classification: LCC LB3430.5 .N38 2022 (print) | LCC LB3430.5 (ebook) |
   DDC 303.3/24--dc23/eng/20220511
LC record available at https://lccn.loc.gov/2021061008
LC ebook record available at https://lccn.loc.gov/2021061009

Solution Tree
Jeffrey C. Jones, CEO
Edmund M. Ackerman, President

Solution Tree Press
President and Publisher: Douglas M. Rife
Associate Publisher: Sarah Payne-Mills
Managing Production Editor: Kendra Slayton
Editorial Director: Todd Brakke
Art Director: Rian Anderson
Copy Chief: Jessi Finn
Senior Production Editor: Laurel Hecker
Content Development Specialist: Amy Rubenstein
Acquisitions Editor: Sarah Jubar
Copy Editor: Mark Hain

Acknowledgments

I would like to acknowledge the many educators who have impacted my life as a person and a professional. The collective efforts of my parents, educators, educational leaders, and family have allowed me to fully experience education in a way that provides opportunities to share. I would also like to acknowledge my wife, Tylee Navo; my mother, Laura Orozco; my father, Mark Navo; my stepfather, Cecilio Orozco; and my sons, Kennedy, Britton, and Trent Navo, for their patience, belief, inspiration, and support as I took on the dream of sharing my experiences in this publication.

—Matt Navo

This book is the culmination of work completed by many educators working tirelessly to serve students and families. I have been inspired by incredible educators focused on ensuring every student experiences success. These educators opened their hearts, minds, and classroom doors with willingness to reflect on current instructional practices and find ways to continually improve. Through their efforts, pitfalls, and celebrations, they provided a roadmap to create schools and classrooms where individual students have their experiences valued, their strengths acknowledged, their educational needs met, and their curiosity cultivated. I am eternally grateful to my husband, Kim Williams; my daughters, Madison and Mckenna; and my mom, Cecilia Allen, for their unwavering support.

—Amy Williams

Solution Tree Press would like to thank the following reviewers:

Faith Cole
MTSS Director
Oak Park Elementary
    School District 97
Oak Park, Illinois

Cathy DeSalvo
MTSS-B Supervisor
Omaha Public Schools
Omaha, Nebraska

Edward Gigliotti
Adjunct Instructor, School
    of Leadership and
    Education Sciences
University of San Diego
    San Diego, California

Caroline Racine Gilles
MTSS Director
Madison Metropolitan
    School District
Madison, Wisconsin

David Hain
RTI/MTSS Coordinator
Lake Forest Schools
Lake Forest, Illinois

Laura Hesson
Washington County School
    District Board Member
Washington County
    School District
St. George, Utah

Adam Kent
Assistant Principal
Fort Dodge Senior High
Fort Dodge, Iowa

Peter Marshall
Education Consultant
Burlington, Ontario

Visit **go.SolutionTree.com/schoolimprovement** to download the free reproducibles in this book.

Table of Contents

Reproducibles are in italics.

About the Authors

 **Matt Navo** is the executive director of the California Collaborative for Educational Excellence. He helps districts and schools develop strategies, structures, policies, and practices that assist in closing the achievement gap for all students.

Matt specializes in aligning systems for building capacity and continuous improvement, building collaborative cultures, and establishing coherent and efficient systems for closing the achievement gap. He also works with the National Center for Systemic Improvement (NCSI), collaborating with state education departments and local district leaders on building improvement methodologies and continuous-improvement frameworks.

Matt has experience as a special education elementary and secondary teacher, counselor, resource teacher, junior high learning director, high school assistant principal, elementary principal, alternative education principal, director of special education, area administrator, and superintendent. He was the governor's appointee for California's Advisory Commission on Special Education (ACSE) from 2014 to 2016, and the governor's appointee to the California Collaborative for Educational Excellence from 2016 to 2017. He was the governor's 2019 appointee for the California State Board of Education and formerly served as the director of systems transformation at WestEd's Center for Prevention and Early Intervention.

Matt has been a keynote speaker at numerous conferences on system improvement across the state of California and was a contributor to the *ONE SYSTEM: Reforming Education to Serve All Students* report of California's Statewide Task Force on Special Education in 2015. As superintendent, Matt's school district was recognized for various achievements such as *Process and Protest—California: How Are Districts Engaging Stakeholders in LCAP Development?* and was honored as a California District of Distinction in 2018.

Matt received a bachelor's degree in education and a master's degree in special education from California State University, Fresno. He holds a professional administrative credential, a multiple-subject teaching credential, and a supplemental credential with an autism emphasis.

 **Amy Williams, EdD,** is a program manager for California Education Partners. She has twenty-four years of experience in education as a coordinator of inclusive services and supports, K–8 principal, special education program manager, school psychologist, and teacher. She leads district-to-district collaboration teams and serves as a coach for participating districts in supporting and building capacity to lead improvement work within districts.

As the coordinator of inclusive services for Sanger Unified School District in Fresno County, California, Amy developed and established the district's multitiered system of supports (MTSS). This process involved setting up the systems and structures to meet the needs of all students, developing a coherent system using data to align initiatives and resources, and using continuous improvement to set up a process for districtwide student improvement outcomes. She is experienced in working with district administrators, principals, and teachers in developing an understanding of how to work with diverse learners, building collaborative teams and cultures, and establishing coherent and aligned systems.

Amy specializes in working with districts and schools in developing, implementing, and supporting initiatives such as MTSS, response to intervention (RTI), positive behavioral interventions and supports (PBIS), and social-emotional learning (SEL). She has worked toward access and equity for all students through Universal Design for Learning (UDL). She has experience in both special and general education, giving her a wide lens and varied perspectives to support all learners within an organization.

As principal, she led Sanger Unified School District's Quail Lake Environmental Charter School to achieve the California Distinguished Schools, National Schools to Watch, PBIS Gold School, and Bonner Center's Virtues and Character awards.

Amy earned a bachelor's degree in psychology, a multiple-subject teaching credential, and an education administration credential from California State University, Fresno; a master's degree in education and a pupil-services credential in school psychology from Fresno Pacific University; and a doctorate in educational leadership from California State University, Fresno, where she researched teachers' perspectives on implementing UDL.

To book Matt Navo or Amy Williams for professional development, contact pd@SolutionTree.com.

Introduction

As the field of education increasingly demands evidence-based supports and interventions that help all students succeed, the concept of *multitiered system of supports* (MTSS) has become a critical part of the discussion on how schools and districts can meaningfully address the education system's inequities. The Every Student Succeeds Act (ESSA) of 2015 defines MTSS as "a comprehensive continuum of evidence-based, systemic practices to support a rapid response to students' needs, with regular observation to facilitate data-based instructional decision making." This definition calls out several features of MTSS.

- **A continuum of practice:** The intensity of supports increases with students' needs.

- **Rapid response to students' needs:** Educators put supports in place immediately after identifying a student need.

- **Regular data use:** Educators collect and review student data in a timely, consistent manner and use those data to inform decision making to address student needs.

These are the basic characteristics of an effective MTSS framework. If schools and districts are to build and sustain an MTSS framework, leaders will need to promote the practice of using data to create a continuum of practices that support students' educational needs in a timely manner (Rogers, Smith, Buffum, & Mattos, 2020). These characteristics—a continuum of practice, rapid response, and consistent data use—are deeply interconnected. In MTSS, educators provide supports of varying intensity to respond to students' academic and behavioral needs. They adjust those supports up or down the continuum as soon as they identify challenges or improvements. MTSS requires data as the primary driver for adjusting supports and services. In other words, educators regularly assess all students and use the results to determine what supports they need. Educators must use evidence-based intervention and support practices (that is, strategies that researchers have found to be effective) and data (such as assessment results) to monitor how well those practices are working for their individual students.

MTSS is more than a check-the-boxes framework; it requires creating a systemic way to develop schoolwide strategies and holistic perspectives (Rogers et al., 2020). Often, schools or districts implement new educational programs or initiatives in isolation with just a few teachers or leaders. This siloed approach often results in failed efforts and initiative fatigue. Instead, MTSS implementation is designed to incorporate all aspects of how students experience school, from how the bus driver interacts with students as they are picked up and driven to school, how staff and students interact in and outside the classroom, how school aides respond to students, to how students engage in after-school activities. MTSS teams consider all aspects of a student's school experience when designing supports, including when and how supports are best delivered to students.

These primary characteristics may seem generally familiar to school teams and as a result one might assume that everyone is already building an MTSS framework in basically the same way. What you will find in the field, however, is far from coherent and consistent. The MTSS process takes many forms and requires quite a bit of trust among all involved, especially since questions of equity are at the heart of the matter (McCart & Miller, 2020). In different states, provinces, and districts, you will find different definitions and structures of what MTSS is and is not.

Table I.1 displays eleven MTSS definitions, highlighting the varied uses of the concept and approaches in different places.

Table I.1: MTSS Definitions

State or Province	MTSS Definition
California	"MTSS is an integrated, comprehensive framework that focuses on CCSS, core instruction, differentiated learning, student-centered learning, individualized student needs, and the alignment of systems necessary for all students' academic, behavioral, and social success" (California Department of Education, 2020).
Colorado	MTSS "is defined as a prevention-based framework of team-driven data-based problem solving for improving the outcomes of every student through family, school, and community partnering and a layered continuum of evidence-based practices applied at the classroom, school, district, region, and state level" (Colorado Department of Education, n.d.).
Florida	MTSS "involves the systematic use of multi-source assessment data to most efficiently allocate resources in order to improve learning for all students, through integrated academic and behavioral supports. To ensure efficient use of resources, schools begin with the identification of trends and patterns using school-wide and grade-level data. Students who need instructional intervention beyond what is provided universally for positive behavior or academic content areas are equipped with targeted, supplemental interventions delivered individually or in small groups at increasing levels of intensity. This system is characterized by a continuum of integrated academic and behavior supports reflecting the need for students to have fluid access to instruction and supports of varying intensity levels" (Florida Department of Education, n.d.).
Illinois	"MTSS is a framework for continuous improvement that is systemic, prevention-focused, and data-informed, providing a coherent continuum of supports responsive to meet the needs of ALL learners" (Illinois MTSS Network, n.d.).
Kansas	MTSS "is a set of evidence-based practices implemented across a system to meet the needs of all learners. Kansas MTSS and Alignment builds a system of prevention, early intervention, and supports to ensure that all students are learning from the instruction. Kansas MTSS and Alignment establishes a system that intentionally focuses on leadership, professional learning, and an empowering culture and content areas of reading, mathematics, behavior, and social-emotional learning" (Kansas State Department of Education, 2019, p. 1).

Massachusetts	"MTSS is a framework designed to meet the needs of all students by ensuring that schools optimize data-driven decision making, progress monitoring, and evidence-based supports and strategies with increasing intensity to sustain student growth. MTSS is not just about tiered interventions, but rather how all the systems in a school or district fit together to ensure a high quality education for all students" (Massachusetts Department of Elementary and Secondary Education, n.d., p. 2).
Michigan	MTSS "is a comprehensive framework comprised of a collection of research-based strategies designed to meet the individual needs and assets of the whole child. MTSS intentionally interconnects the education, health, and human service systems in support of successful learners, schools, centers, and community outcomes. The five essential components of MTSS are inter-related and complementary. The MTSS framework provides schools and districts with an efficient way to organize resources to support educators in the implementation of effective practices with fidelity so that all learners succeed" (Michigan Department of Education, n.d.).
New York	"MTSS is a framework for both academic and behavioral instruction. MTSS is grounded in the belief that all students can learn, and all school professionals are responsive to the academic and behavioral needs of all students. MTSS focuses on evidence-based practices, relies on student progress data to inform instructional decisions, and ensures that each student, based on their unique needs, receives the level and type of support necessary to be successful" (New York State Education Department, n.d.).
Nova Scotia	"MTSS is an integrated school-wide approach (universal, focused, intensive) which provides a structure for effective instruction, assessment, and support for all students. It requires the collaboration and coordinated efforts of students, teachers, support staff, educational leaders, families, guardians, parents and community partners in providing appropriate programs, settings, supports, and services" (Government of Nova Scotia, n.d.).
Oregon	MTSS "is an integrated, systemic framework designed to use data-based problem-solving to respond to the needs of all students. MTSS aligns school systems to efficiently use resources while focusing on improving learning outcomes for all students. This is accomplished in an MTSS by focusing on effective core instruction (in both academics and for social/emotional) followed by evidence based and increasingly intensive or 'tiered' interventions" (Oregon Department of Education, n.d.).
Tennessee	"The MTSS framework encompasses RTI² in addition to Response to Instruction and Intervention for Behavior (RTI2-B) and other models of support. Working in concert, these programs complement each other and can better address the needs of the whole student. Neither academic nor non-academic concerns should be considered in isolation as the two often interact to contribute to a student's strengths and needs. . . . The MTSS framework offers the potential to create needed systematic change by districts and schools through the alignment of initiatives, supports, and resources to address the needs of *all* students" (Tennessee Department of Education, 2018, p. 4, 6).

Beyond universal foundational elements like tiered supports and data-driven practices, MTSS definitions become increasingly contextualized to the organization's needs. (We use the term *organization* throughout the book to refer generally to schools, districts, and other education agencies, since MTSS can be implemented at various levels.) A state, province, or school district may emphasize the intensive professional learning required for these efforts. Educators in another district may be working with historically underserved students and include the foundational belief systems that need to change in order to achieve the essential goals of MTSS. As teams learn more about what MTSS is and what their system requires, they use that knowledge and understanding to inform, develop, and refine their own MTSS definition. This learning results in various MTSS definitions with the same foundational elements but including other features.

The variance in definitions has proliferated as more schools and districts have adopted MTSS. But at its core, MTSS works specifically to help educators better understand students' unique learning needs. Understanding the various assets students bring in conjunction with their learning needs provides educators a lens of educational equity through which to look as they consider research-based practices and teaching methods to enhance student learning. The capacity to understand student assets and address student learning needs positions educators to see more clearly what may or may not be working to close learning gaps and inequities in education. Meeting students where they are in their individual learning journeys better positions educational systems to accelerate learning to close achievement gaps for all students, especially students who are historically underserved.

Fundamentally, MTSS involves designing learning opportunities that maximize inclusivity and access for all students while minimizing barriers and structures that marginalize individual students or groups, and it provides a framework supporting educators' efforts to address disparities between student groups (Mercado, 2018). MTSS is based on a tiered approach to student support. These supports generally fall into three tiers. Tier 1 is the school program all students receive or engage in, sometimes referred to as universal core instruction. Tier 2 is designed for students who struggle to meet the expectations of Tier 1; they receive targeted small-group instruction with evidence-based interventions that address their assessed needs in order to prevent them from falling further behind. Tier 3 is more intensive and addresses more severe gaps in students' learning by further reducing the numbers of students in an intervention group and increasing the time they receive support customized to meet each student's unique learning needs. Educators and experts often use a pyramid to depict the three tiers of support, as shown in figure I.1.

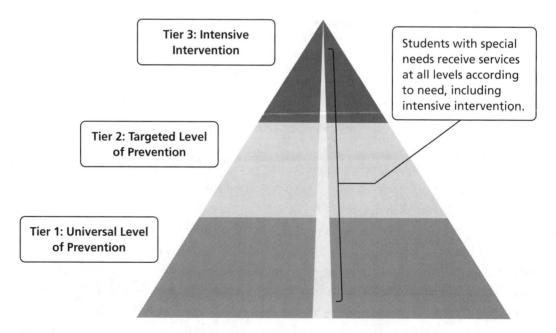

Figure I.1: The MTSS framework.

The tiered approach of MTSS moves away from a single standard practice that results in many students failing to a responsive system that adjusts to the variability of student needs (Rose, 2016; Sailor, 2015). MTSS reframes the debate over what works in education with the potential to shift away from classification and labeling (for example, general education and special education) toward a more timely, positive, and responsive approach that results in social-emotional and academic gains for all students, including those requiring intensive supports and services (Sailor, 2017).

This shift in perspective provides a new approach for how educators measure potential and identify students' strengths and talents (Sailor, 2017). As a result, a number of states and provinces have adopted MTSS as a framework to address inequity and improve student outcomes. States and provinces implementing MTSS have chosen to be responsive to student needs rather than reactive; they have chosen to adopt a way of thinking and doing to ensure every student receives the appropriate level of support when needed. Figure I.2 (page 6) shows a map of the adoption of MTSS and other tiered models in the United States and Canada. This map highlights the fact that the majority of U.S. states have specifically identified MTSS as their primary framework for addressing student needs.

It is important to note that many region-specific models are based on inclusive practices and tiered supports similar to those of MTSS, though the education agencies refer to their systems by a different term. States and provinces also consider other student-support frameworks like response to intervention (RTI) and positive behavioral interventions and supports (PBIS) to be distinct from MTSS. In the book *Integrated Multi-Tiered Systems of Support: Blending RTI and PBIS*, researchers and authors Kent McIntosh and Steve Goodman (2016) state:

> Given the extensive spread and effectiveness of these two approaches [RTI and PBIS], there has been considerable informal discussion of how these approaches could be integrated into a coherent, unified system, sometimes referred to as *multi-tiered systems of support* or *MTSS*. (p. 5)

Many education agencies include RTI and PBIS, along with other essential elements, *within* their MTSS frameworks. In a scan of MTSS frameworks across various states and provinces, we found RTI commonly described as a tiered *academic* support. It was also common to find PBIS described as a tiered *behavioral* support and noted as an important practice. In other words, PBIS and RTI are elements of many MTSS frameworks. Although PBIS and RTI are both models that can be part of an MTSS framework, MTSS is not just PBIS and RTI. MTSS integrates and expands both frameworks beyond their specific focus to include academics, behavior, and social-emotional learning; leadership; community and family engagement; and instructional frameworks, all of which enhance and support RTI and PBIS.

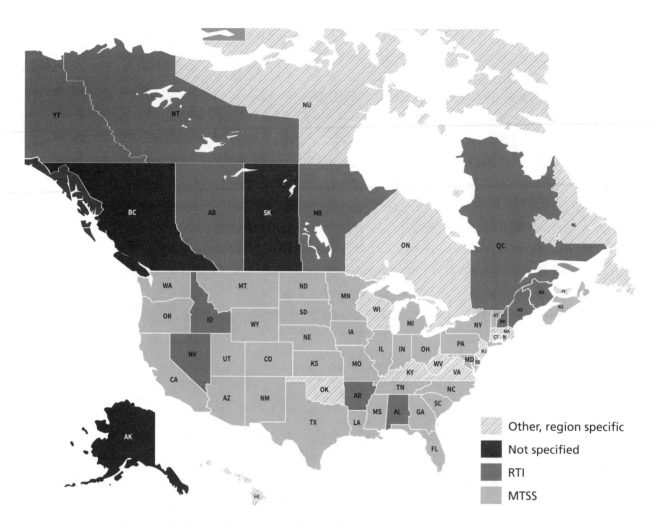

Source: Bailey, 2019; Gouvernement du Québec, 2016; Government of Alberta, 2018; Government of British Columbia, 2022; Government of Manitoba, n.d.; Government of Northwest Territories, 2017; Government of Nunavut, n.d.; New Brunswick Department of Education and Early Childhood Development, 2015; Newfoundland and Labrador Department of Education, 2020; Ontario Ministry of Education, 2013; Saskatchewan Ministry of Education, 2020; Whitley & Hollweck, 2020; Yee, 2020.

Figure I.2: Adoption of MTSS and other frameworks in North America.

This shift toward a description of MTSS that incorporates RTI and PBIS as subcomponents is evident in the movement toward broader inclusion of various evidence-based practices and initiatives. In addition to RTI and PBIS, the following are common essential elements from different states' and provinces' MTSS frameworks.

- A tiered approach to address student academic, behavioral, and social-emotional needs

- Data-driven decision making

- Evidence-based practices

- Continuous-improvement methodologies

- Shared leadership and collaboration

- Problem-solving teams to correctly identify student support needs

- Intervention-review meetings

- Stakeholder engagement and involvement

- Equity

- Universal Design for Learning (UDL)

Although this list is not all-inclusive, it does identify common elements that states and provinces have deemed most essential to include in their MTSS frameworks. It also demonstrates the variety of elements that has led to the variability in MTSS implementation.

That variability creates questions for educators: How do we construct and implement the critical features of MTSS as defined in our state, province, school, or district? Are there other essential elements necessary to include? How do other evidence-based initiatives such as RTI, PBIS, and UDL interact with MTSS? What about the role of leadership? This book helps answer such questions by distilling broad descriptions into simpler systems and processes for building an effective MTSS framework. Throughout the chapters, we demystify MTSS and the implementation process to help you ensure all students succeed.

How to Use This Book

As general education and special education practitioners, we have experienced the gap between the research and theory and the real implementation of MTSS. We have applied various MTSS ideas, theories, models, and research and have experienced successes, challenges, and failures. The purpose of this book is to provide all preK–12 educators with a comprehensive and pragmatic process to shift their current organizational system to a more coherent and aligned system reflective of an effective MTSS framework. This book's primary audience is school and district leaders and administrators who are interested in understanding a simple yet impactful foundational structure for MTSS. We also believe that teachers, teacher teams, teacher leaders, school board members, and parents should learn what MTSS is and how to build a basic MTSS framework. Anyone responsible for building, participating in, and contributing to MTSS can use this book to better understand the structures that ultimately improve student outcomes. By reading this book, you will understand the opportunities for each staff member to contribute to the successful implementation of MTSS.

Chapter 1 lays out the four parts of our MTSS framework: (1) collaborative leadership, (2) universal access, (3) a continuum of tiered supports, and (4) data-based decision making. We explain how you might approach the information in this book and provide insights as to how we move from theory to practice. The four subsequent chapters each detail one of the four parts of our model and the key components within it.

Chapter 2 outlines the foundational role of collaborative leadership. Team structures and processes, such as the professional learning community (PLC) process, serve as the foundation of successful MTSS implementation and sustainability. In this chapter, we explain why collaboration is essential to MTSS, define MTSS improvement teams and why they are crucial, and present universal communication strategies for conveying the purpose of MTSS.

In chapter 3, we build understanding around the concept of *universal access*. We share the value of UDL for core instruction. Based on research in learner differences and effective teaching practices and taking advantage of the capacity of new technologies, UDL provides an instructional approach that creates a more robust and accessible learning experience for all students (Rose & Meyer, 2006). We address how universal supports, screening, and monitoring provide information on students' progress through tiers of support and how to manage student tiers of support. We also cover how universal supports, screening, and monitoring help educator teams align and prioritize curriculum standards, assessments, tiers of intervention, data, deep collaboration, and problem solving.

In chapter 4, we address a continuum of tiered supports for students' academic, behavioral, and social-emotional needs. This chapter also focuses on using evidence-based practices. We provide an inventory tool for this component that allows teams to evaluate how the system aligns resources, people, time, and funding.

In chapter 5, we move to data-based decision making, the processes required to build a sustainable system focused on student performance data. We prioritize understanding quality assessments, introduce an assessment inventory, discuss data-discussion calendars, and present a data-analysis protocol for collaborative teams.

To link all the parts of the framework together, organizations must use continuous-improvement processes. Chapter 6 discusses how continuous improvement is essential to developing an MTSS framework. Continuous improvement means applying action research to effectively evaluate current organizational characteristics, identify gaps, and design plans to improve essential elements of your MTSS framework.

Each chapter includes four practical tools.

1. **Case study:** We present a case study as a real-world example of how teams and organizations might experience building an MTSS framework. Though fictional, these case studies are based on our experiences in schools and districts.

2. **Team activity:** MTSS is a collaborative effort relying on multiple perspectives and viewpoints to tackle students' educational needs. Each chapter's team activity guides you to consider how the chapter content applies to your organizational context and reflect on your team's implementation efforts. The questions allow your team to assess its current reality, determine what you need to change, and identify barriers.

3. **Component audit:** The component audit provides a vehicle for your team to analyze its own MTSS implementation of each component described in the chapter. Completing the component audit will help you assess your current state and develop a starting point for next steps.

4. **MTSS action plan:** Finally, the MTSS action plan combines the results of the team activity and the component audit. You will plan out and track your next steps for each part of the model to create a comprehensive plan for your school or district.

You may approach this book's topics in sequence, moving from one chapter to the next either as a book study or for systematic implementation. If you prefer, you may choose to read through the entire book first and then pick your starting point of highest need to begin implementation. Once you have read and completed the activities provided in this book, you will have the essential organizational structures for building an MTSS framework, including the skills, tools, and resources to ensure implementation and sustainability. To establish a broad understanding, chapter 1 provides an overview of our customizable MTSS framework and its core components.

Chapter 1

A Comprehensive MTSS Model

William Edwards Deming, considered by many to be the father of continuous improvement, is quoted as saying that education is a field characterized by "miracle goals and no methods" (as cited in Bryk, 2020, p. 3). This quote reflects the idea that if we fail to develop effective improvement strategies, the results we want will be unlikely to materialize. In our experience, when a system fails to produce improvement, people tend to blame the user (in education, this means parents, teachers, leaders, or even students). However, we argue that this failure to improve is often symptomatic of poorly constructed methods or approaches. As described in the introduction, the numerous manifestations of MTSS can cause confusion for educators trying to implement this framework. Building an MTSS framework is complicated. It involves the voices of multiple educational partners, community members, educators, and researchers. Often, the complexity of this endeavor prompts users to respond in one of two ways: (1) we are not ready for this, or (2) we have already done this. Rather than blaming the user, we endeavor to design a better system where all users of the system can find success.

In this chapter, we present a four-part MTSS framework that includes the core elements yet is simple enough to understand and customize for various contexts. To lay the foundation for what we cover in this chapter, we define *MTSS* for our purposes as a holistic framework that uses collaborative leadership structures to create a universally accessible instructional framework and includes a continuum of tiered supports that depend on evidence-based practices and data analysis to improve student outcomes. This definition encapsulates the four elements essential for building an MTSS framework that we discuss in this chapter.

Our MTSS Framework

We have created a comprehensive model of MTSS that hinges on four key elements.

1. Collaborative leadership

2. Universal access

3. Continuum of tiered supports

4. Data-based decision making

These elements do not function in isolation; rather, they should work together so they integrate and complement each other. Continuous-improvement processes tie all the elements together, allowing educator teams to evaluate any innovation using data for improving student outcomes. At the heart of MTSS is a student-centered mindset. The work of MTSS is putting student outcomes and needs at the core of all elements of the framework. In other words, teams, schools, and districts working toward a strong MTSS framework must keep their students at the center of all the work they do. Figure 1.1 shows a visual of this model.

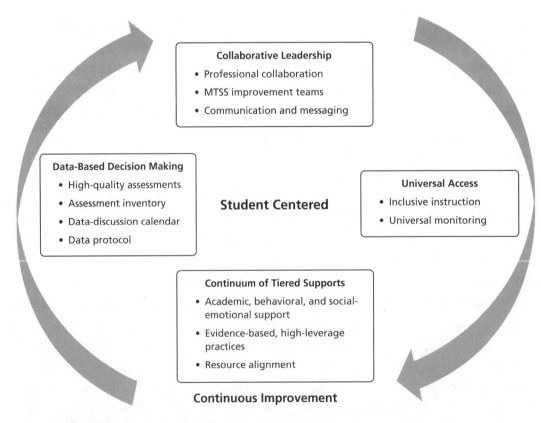

Figure 1.1: MTSS framework.

This holistic framework, with its prioritized elements for MTSS, is an antidote to the myriad MTSS definitions, varying implementations, and confusion from educational practitioners. Our definition for MTSS provides a basic model that will help administrators align their school systems and resources (people, time, and funding) in an effort to maximize student achievement. It is not overly complicated but it is comprehensive enough to meet the urgent call for equitable educational outcomes and address all students' needs as it reflects best practices for building an MTSS framework. The following sections provide a brief introduction of each element of our MTSS framework. We further explain each component within the four key elements in chapters 2–5.

Collaborative Leadership

Our framework provides schools and districts with the essential elements needed to implement MTSS effectively while encouraging educators to contextualize aspects of MTSS to their organization. This collective effort demands leadership and collaboration. MTSS implementation requires multiple stakeholders working in sync. Collaborative leadership structures define *when*, *what*, and *how* all those in a school or district engage in building and evaluating an MTSS framework. Collaborative leadership includes three essential components.

1. Professional collaboration

2. MTSS improvement teams

3. Communication and messaging

Professional Collaboration

To build an MTSS framework, you must first establish and build a strong culture of professional collaboration. Collaboration is a key component of successful MTSS implementation. Teachers will need to work interdependently to provide universal instruction, identify student needs, and support students through interventions. Leaders, specialists, and other staff must also collaborate in service of students. If your school or district does not have a strong collaborative model and culture, we encourage you and your colleagues to strengthen that foundation, which will benefit the overall development of an MTSS framework.

In this book, we recommend the professional learning communities process as an effective method of professional collaboration. While we focus our discussion on PLCs, we also acknowledge that various organizations may use other collaborative models. PLC architects and experts Richard DuFour, Rebecca DuFour, Robert Eaker, Thomas W. Many, and Mike Mattos (2016) define a PLC as:

> An ongoing process in which educators work collaboratively in recurring cycles of collective inquiry and action research to achieve better results for the students they serve. PLCs work under the assumption that the key to improved learning for students is continuous job-embedded learning for educators. (p. 10)

PLCs are guided by three big ideas and four critical questions. The three big ideas are as follows (DuFour et al., 2016).

1. A focus on learning

2. A collaborative culture and collective responsibility

3. A results orientation

The following four critical questions are the focus of the work within a PLC (DuFour et al., 2016).

1. What is it we want our students to know and be able to do?

2. How will we know if each student has learned it?

3. How will we respond when some students do not learn it?

4. How will we extend the learning for students who have demonstrated proficiency?

Having a culture of professional collaboration that focuses on clearly identified student learning needs and outcomes provides the foundation for building a robust MTSS framework.

MTSS Improvement Teams

MTSS is a continual process of refinement, never stagnant, always needing to be improved, enhanced, and readdressed. To do this work of continuous improvement, leaders need to thoughtfully select staff members to form an MTSS improvement team. MTSS improvement teams work in a cycle of continuous improvement through reflection and action. They identify problems, establish clear goals, formulate changes, and test those changes. The team's focus is improving the system rather than making decisions or implementing quick fixes. MTSS improvement teams are the core to building the organizational MTSS framework as school teams grapple with challenges, changes, and improvements that best meet student needs. MTSS work requires broad collaborative educational voices, efforts, and perspectives from different team members who understand and are willing to engage in continuous-improvement methods. We recommend including staff members with expertise in RTI, PBIS, general and special education, and instructional coaching, as well as classified and teacher-support staff. These various perspectives are critical to improving MTSS because including various perspectives forms a more collective effort and commitment for MTSS.

Communication and Messaging

The third component in collaborative leadership structures is communicating information about MTSS throughout your organization and the community. Thoughtfully developing consistent, strategic messaging improves stakeholder engagement, confidence in the motives, and collective efforts toward implementation. At the core of messaging for MTSS are *Why MTSS?* and *How do we do it?* More specifically, leaders should have answers to the following questions.

- How is MTSS different from what we are already doing?

- Why is MTSS good for the students we serve?

- How will MTSS affect us as a team?

- How will we get this done?

Communicating the why and the how of MTSS is critical if teams are going to get started on the right foot.

Universal Access

Universal access refers to the fact that MTSS is about all students. It is not only for students who struggle academically or students who display problem behaviors. It is essential for each and every student. It supports those who need additional resources as well as those who need accelerated learning. The foundation of MTSS is that all students receive high-quality initial instruction and classroom learning environments. Universal access minimizes barriers students and teachers may encounter while teaching and learning the grade-level standards. Within this element of the framework, we consider the components of inclusive instruction and universal monitoring, both of which are essential to building universal access.

Inclusive Instruction

Classroom teachers in a school using the MTSS framework should proactively consider how instruction can meet all students' needs. In other words, general instruction should be flexible and seek to accommodate many types of learners. Inclusive classrooms have clear goals but flexible means of instruction. As an example, if the goal is to understand the causes and effects of the U.S. Civil War, there are multiple ways a student might demonstrate that understanding to meet the standard. A variety of on-ramps to learning and demonstrating learning better accommodate students' strengths and learning needs as compared to a very narrow assignment that asks all students to demonstrate their learning in the same way.

Our preferred model for inclusive instruction is UDL, which provides instructional principles for educators to use in designing lessons, learning spaces, and experiences. Education consultants Peggy Coyne, Miriam Evans, and Joanne Karger (2017) state that UDL "addresses the natural variability of learners by increasing flexibility and reducing barriers in instruction" (p. 4). By creating inclusive environments, teachers can effectively meet all students' needs, specifically dual-language learners and students with identified disabilities (Howard, 2006; Rao, Smith, & Lowrey, 2017). UDL focuses on pedagogy, systems, and structures and not the student characteristics (Sailor & McCart, 2014). For these reasons, we introduce UDL as the framework for creating universally accessible curriculum and instruction.

Universal Monitoring

Continuing the theme of universality, MTSS involves collecting data on all students' learning and behavior, not only those who struggle. Universal screening and progress monitoring of performance and growth provide key data on indicators of student progress. These data allow educators to proactively design interventions and consistently monitor their impact on student growth. What makes these assessments universal is that all students receive them at designated times during the school year to ensure all students' strengths and challenges are addressed and supported.

Continuum of Tiered Supports

MTSS is a tiered approach to supporting student improvement in academics, behavior, and social-emotional learning. As students present varying degrees of need for support and services, supports increase in accordance with each student's needs. Universal supports in Tier 1 treat all students as eligible for support through prevention and remediation structures. Tier 2 supports target specific skill deficits for students at risk of falling behind. Tier 3 is designed for students already demonstrating significant skill deficits and requiring intensive intervention to remediate deficiencies (McIntosh & Goodman, 2016). MTSS is in service of preventing students from falling further behind both academically and behaviorally (McIntosh & Goodman, 2016). Our experience provides some insights on how to begin designing a tiered support system, and we consider both the challenges and the ways to get started in the following sections.

Academic, Behavioral, and Social-Emotional Supports

The tiered supports of MTSS include evidence-based interventions, prevention-minded approaches, increased intensity based on student need, consistent universal screening for interventions, use of problem-solving and data-based decision-making models, teaming, and continuous improvement. MTSS focuses on both academics and behavior, including social-emotional supports, which serve complementary roles to provide a continuum of supports with the whole student in mind.

Evidence-Based and High-Leverage Practices

The use of evidence-based practices ensures that the interventions and instructional strategies educators implement meet a standard of effectiveness based on respected research and publications (McIntosh & Goodman, 2016). Unfortunately, many common practices schools use are not evidence based and do not always improve student outcomes. This part of our MTSS framework prioritizes strategies that have been proven effective to ensure that educators use the best methods and approaches to improve student results. We especially highlight high-leverage practices—best practices that complement and support broader evidence-based practices.

Resource Alignment

MTSS requires educators to shift how they think about and distribute resources to meet student needs. In the urgency to close achievement gaps and ensure students develop necessary academic, behavioral, and social-emotional skills, educators need to re-evaluate how they spend resources such as time, people, and funding. Taking an inventory of resources helps identify current priorities and re-establish new priorities focused on student improvement. Administrators using student data need to prioritize and align these valuable resources on actions, initiatives, and projects that improve student achievement. Aligned resources allow for an all-hands-on-deck approach to addressing barriers in the system. For example, imagine a principal meeting with sixth-grade teams to review student achievement on literacy outcomes. The data indicate that a disproportionate number of students are struggling with reading comprehension. The teams further break down the data to find students are struggling specifically with textual evidence. As a result, the principal uses funds to purchase evidence-backed resources related to using textual evidence and requests that district coaches provide professional learning and coaching to support instruction in the classroom. At the core of this alignment of resources are student data, which drive how funds are spent to support staff and students.

When an organization is not aligning resources, there is a disconnect between student needs and how the organization spends time and money. Perhaps, instead of following student data to determine that a new evidence-based phonics program is the best use of resources, the aforementioned principal simply looks at what programs the school already owns and suggests teachers increase the time and duration of use. This approach implies that the solution is using an ineffective phonics program longer and more frequently. Ultimately, decisions about time, people, and money affect students.

Data-Based Decision Making

MTSS requires that educators base decisions about instructional strategies and curriculum on data. The skills and practice of making data-based decisions are a prerequisite to the problem-solving model of an MTSS framework. Only with data can effective decisions and discussion take place. At minimum, teams must implement data-based decision-making protocols to facilitate discussions and analyses of student data. This requires access to data in ways that allow educators to not only uncover areas of ineffective results, but also highlight positive results that others can learn from. The consistent use of data helps teams evaluate their efficiency and effectiveness and identify areas for improvement. Aligning teams' efforts begins by asking simply, "What areas do the data indicate we need to improve?"

What Makes Our Framework Different

This book lays out the steps needed to build an MTSS framework that removes the fog of confusion around what an MTSS framework is, what it must consist of, and most importantly, how a team can continually refine its practices. Continuous improvement brings the theory of application of MTSS into practice by ensuring that those within the system are continually evaluating the effectiveness of implementation and student outcomes.

In traditional models, the evaluation of practice, ideas, innovation, and changes occurs at the end of the year, semester, quarter, or trimester. Our MTSS framework monitors effectiveness of implementation more frequently through ongoing rapid cycles of improvement and evaluation. By studying the impact of changes and adjusting accordingly in a constant feedback loop, you will learn which efforts efficiently result in student improvement and which do not. You will also avoid the common trap of simply pursuing the latest instructional or curricular trend (the "shiny new object") that often distracts from the real and hard work of understanding systems and building an effective MTSS framework.

Summary

This chapter summarizes the four elements of our MTSS framework: (1) collaborative leadership, (2) universal access, (3) a continuum of tiered supports, and (4) data-based decision making. We describe the components within each of the four essential elements and what is necessary to build a student-centered MTSS framework. As we move forward, each chapter presents more specific strategies for each of the four elements in order to provide teams a starting point and suggested approaches.

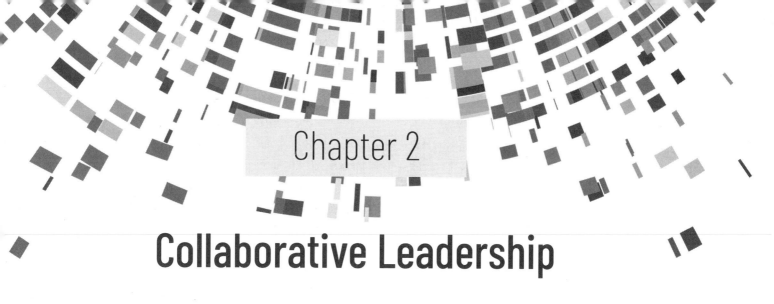

Chapter 2

Collaborative Leadership

Education experts and authors Anthony Muhammad and Luis F. Cruz (2019) describe leadership as "the ability to use influence to improve organizational productivity" (p. 2). Influencing an organization is the mission of educational leaders' work, and sharing leadership responsibilities helps ensure the school system improves student outcomes. To organize shared leadership for MTSS, schools need *collaborative leadership structures*—processes that promote collaborative work in pursuit of improved student outcomes and create a communication feedback loop between various educators focused on student improvement. Such organizational structures define how to conduct specific activities to achieve the goals and objectives of the organization (Bolman & Deal, 2013).

This chapter presents the collaborative leadership structures for building an MTSS framework. We prioritize three components.

1. Professional collaboration

2. MTSS improvement teams

3. Communication and messaging

We share how all three of these components are essential for district and school teams to form the right collaborative leadership structures to improve organizational alignment and outcomes for their students. These structures are necessary for doing the difficult work of building a holistic MTSS framework.

Professional Collaboration

Professional collaboration works from a stance of interdependency, maximizing each team member's professional strengths to ensure all students meet shared expectations for learning.

In *Learning by Doing*, DuFour and colleagues (2016) summarize the importance of professional collaboration in education.

> John Hattie (2015) contends that the best system leaders create a "collaborative expertise" culture within and between schools. In such a culture, there is clarity regarding the priorities and purpose of the district, an intense focus on student learning, ready access to evidence of student learning that allows educators to intervene for students who are struggling, professional dialogue regarding the effectiveness of different instructional strategies based on evidence of student learning, and recognition of the power of collective wisdom to help teachers have a positive impact on student learning. (p. 243)

A school or district with a culture of professional collaboration is one where teachers convene to discuss student learning. This centralizes student learning needs in the context of guiding questions and beliefs about students' abilities to learn. The very essence of a collaborative culture is its members' focus on and commitment to each student's learning outcomes (DuFour et al., 2016). Professional collaboration requires that all team members share responsibility for learning and working together to improve student learning outcomes.

As mentioned in chapter 1 (page 11), we recommend the PLC process for this work. According to DuFour and colleagues (2016), "When a school or district functions as a PLC, educators within the organization embrace high levels of learning for all students as both the reason the organization exists and the fundamental responsibility of those who work within it" (p. 11). The four critical questions of a PLC direct educators toward improved student learning outcomes (DuFour et al., 2016).

1. What is it we want our students to know and be able to do?

2. How will we know if each student has learned it?

3. How will we respond when some students do not learn it?

4. How will we extend the learning for students who have demonstrated proficiency?

The PLC process organizes all staff into collaborative teams to respond to these questions, which educators need to continually ask as they work to provide a continuum of supports for students.

A PLC anchored by the four critical questions is a supportive foundation for MTSS (DuFour et al., 2016). With its focus on learning and analyzing student data, the PLC process helps teachers establish high-quality core instruction for all students and respond to students' needs. Specifically in a PLC, the first question (What is it we want our students to know and be able to do?) relates to the component of universal access—creating quality core instruction for all. This core instruction is Tier 1 of MTSS, which we explain in more detail in the next chapter. To ensure the effectiveness of Tier 1 instruction, collaborative teams need to analyze student learning data. This analysis leads directly to data-based decision making, which corresponds to the second PLC question (How will we know if each student has learned it?). By analyzing the data, educators can appraise instructional effectiveness and determine what they need to change to improve student outcomes (Bernhardt, 2018).

Analyzing student data also allows teams to effectively identify and distribute tiered support and intervention. This practice relates to MTSS's continuum of tiered support and answers the third and fourth critical questions of a PLC (How will we respond when some students do not learn it? and How will we extend the learning for students who have demonstrated proficiency?).

In building collaborative leadership structures, leaders need to guide their staff away from thinking PLCs are a freestanding program, or a meeting held every so often, or a to-do list (DuFour et al., 2016). The PLC process informs all aspects of educators' work and requires true organizationwide collaboration. The collective commitment of teams to respond to each student's unique learning needs is required in building an MTSS. This effort calls for collaboration and clarity because the work engages multiple teams of educators in using professional expertise in a coordinated way to more effectively design supports for students.

Professional collaboration efforts that serve as the foundation of understanding students' learning needs within an MTSS framework must extend beyond grade-level or content-area teams to a larger school-site and district-level conversation. When grade-level or content-area teams engage in professional collaboration, they should also share and discuss information with the schoolwide MTSS improvement team or leadership team. Those schoolwide teams discuss trends, themes, and practices that are barriers for teachers and students; teams should also discuss practices that enhance teacher and student success. The schoolwide teams should share their discussions, discoveries, and needs with a districtwide MTSS improvement team or leadership team. And ultimately, communication should also flow back the way it came so that silos are broken and the system as a whole benefits from the discussion of student learning.

It's clear that without data-based, learning-focused collaboration as a foundation, teams will be far less prepared to implement an MTSS framework. Without this approach, a school or district will fail to build coordinated, tiered support and intervention plans to meet all students' unique learning needs. Organizations' failure to build these basic interventions often results in students slipping through the cracks and not receiving adequate supports (McIntosh & Goodman, 2016).

If you are part of a school that operates as a PLC or has otherwise achieved schoolwide professional collaboration in service of student learning, you can rest assured that you are on the right track to develop your MTSS framework. For teams that may still be investigating the idea of implementing the PLC process or another professional collaboration model, we hope this section highlights the urgent need for a coordinated effort. Teams that are confident and understand the purpose of their collaboration are ready for the work involved in building and providing universal core instruction, as well as the use of data to identify students for tiered interventions and supports. This understanding happens more effectively when professional collaboration structures such as PLCs are in place because the teams are already focused on and working collectively toward improving student learning outcomes. Regardless of which model you use to guide professional collaboration, the focus and priorities are not on what teachers want to teach, but rather on how students learn.

Beyond professional collaboration of grade-level teams is the collaboration focused on building and improving your MTSS framework. In the next section, we discuss MTSS improvement teams, which form a structure for looking at system-level changes that are necessary for implementing and sustaining an MTSS framework.

MTSS Improvement Teams

Our experience has been that many schools and districts have various teams in place designed to create effective and efficient systems to support students' learning needs. These teams sometimes include leadership teams that monitor and evaluate the overall success of instruction and student outcomes, student study teams that problem solve and determine supports students may need, intervention teams that provide the targeted instruction and monitor the student response to intervention, and behavioral teams that work to improve student engagement and positive interactions within the school day. The bigger the system, usually the more teams. All of these teams are designed to react to something that needs attention within the system. What we have not seen as often in our experience is a team designed to be proactive—a team that investigates problems more deeply, learns to understand the issues fully, and tests changes and solutions before they scale the innovations systemwide. This is the void that the MTSS improvement team fills. The MTSS team analyzes and evaluates student data and helps design and lead the changes needed to improve student outcomes based on that data.

MTSS improvement teams are comprised of educators who focus on understanding how a system works. The goal of this focus on understanding the system is to build a coordinated school- or districtwide response for improving student outcomes. MTSS improvement teams contribute to educators' collective efforts by providing a common language and a framework. Building this capacity requires educators to engage in a systemwide discussion that moves beyond classroom responses to student learning needs to create school- and districtwide responses. Here we discuss who should be on an MTSS improvement team and what the team will do once formed.

Who Should Be on an MTSS Improvement Team

MTSS improvement teams can have more effective conversations about system improvement when they include a cross-section of staff. Members should represent a spectrum of knowledge and experiences from the school or district that promotes understanding of the implementation efforts for MTSS. Team members who are closest to understanding student learning needs, in conjunction with those who understand system barriers, comprise the best improvement teams. For efforts like MTSS to be successful, educators must understand the unique challenges of the school and organization as well as uniquely understand student learning needs. For example, the team should include members with expertise in academic and behavioral interventions, such as RTI and PBIS. These are critical practices under a continuum of tiered supports and interventions for MTSS, discussed in chapter 4 (page 59).

The MTSS improvement team's attributes are what the authors of *Learning to Improve* (Bryk, Gomez, Grunow, & LeMahieu, 2015) call *user and problem focused*. At its most basic level, being user focused means respecting the people who do the work by seeking to understand the problems they confront (Bryk et al., 2015).

We strongly encourage you to build an MTSS improvement team that includes varied practitioner perspectives such as teachers, school psychologists, nonteaching staff, administrators, and even parents. The variety of user perspectives offers unique insights into students' needs. As an example, a district-level MTSS improvement team might include the following members.

- District-level decision maker (such as a superintendent, assistant superintendent, director of curriculum and instruction, or other cabinet-level administrator directly responsible for instructional outcomes)
- Site-level administrator
- Special education teacher, administrator, or support staff
- General education teacher
- Classified staff member, administrator, or support staff (such as a school nurse, chief financial officer, transportation director, or food services director)
- Stakeholder who is invested in the school and community (such as a representative from a local youth program, a parks and recreation director, a community liaison, or a parent leader)

A school-level MTSS improvement team might have the following members.

- Principal (or representative decision maker)
- General education teacher
- Special education teacher
- Classified staff member (such as a school nurse)
- Curriculum coach, trainer, or support person
- Specialized staff member (such as a school psychologist, counselor, or speech and language pathologist)
- District support personnel
- Stakeholder who shares an interest in the work (such as the director of a local childcare facility or a parks and recreation director)

If your school or district already has a team composed of such a variety of stakeholders, you may not need to create a new team, though a shift in the existing team's approach may be necessary to build your MTSS framework.

What an MTSS Improvement Team Does

The most considerable difference between existing teams and an MTSS improvement team is not always their composition but rather the principles by which they function. The difference between the teams we typically see in education and an MTSS improvement team is the distinction between learning and solving. In *Improvement in Action*, Anthony Bryk (2020) indicates, "It is not surprising that a chasm has been widening for some time between our rising aspiration for what we would like schools to carry out and what they are able to routinely achieve" (p. 2). Bryk (2020) goes on to explain that to improve, schools need to be able to answer two big questions.

1. How do educational organizations continuously get better at what they do while recognizing the quickening pace for change?

2. How do we accelerate our learning to improve?

The second question, "How do we accelerate our learning to improve?" is the main distinction between typical teams and improvement teams. Many teams are structured for solving problems, meaning they are focused on finding and implementing a solution as fast as possible. Solving problems often leads to quick changes without clearly understanding the root cause. This approach leads to an overwhelming number of disconnected solutions. Education experts and Carnegie Foundation leaders Anthony S. Bryk, Louis M. Gomez, Alicia Grunow, and Paul G. LeMahieu (2015) term this *solutionitis*—"The propensity to jump quickly on a solution before fully understanding the exact problem to be solved" (p. 24). Improvement teams are structured for learning over time as their primary purpose, requiring a different approach, specifically focused on learning about what works and doesn't work over time. MTSS improvement teams are grounded in the following methods.

*   Using systematic continuous-improvement cycles (see chapter 6, page 117)

*   Interpreting data

*   Understanding and investigating underlying structures or processes that negatively impact student outcomes

*   Testing system improvement ideas and changes for potential scale and spreading of efforts

Creating effective collaborative leadership structures for MTSS requires a shift from traditional thinking and approaches, such as being too reactive, making assumptions around data, and looking at student data in isolation from other factors. An MTSS improvement team instead designs more thoughtful, explicit, and coordinated approaches to student learning needs.

The first step to implementing an MTSS improvement team is for educators to take a different approach to conversation. An MTSS improvement team agenda should be simple and guided by open-ended questions that require profound thought and consideration. The agenda template shown in figure 2.1 can help get your MTSS improvement team agenda started with the right focus. A reproducible version appears at the end of the chapter (page 35).

Agenda Questions	Agenda Discussion Notes
What do the data tell us currently?	District Progress Assessment Scores **Reading** K: 81–88 percent 1: 79–82 percent 2: 82–86 percent 3: 78–87 percent 4: 77–78 percent 5: (missing) 6: 90–95 percent **Mathematics Facts** K: 6–15 percent (addition and subtraction) 1: 35–39 percent (addition and subtraction) 2: 48–58 percent (addition and subtraction) 3: 39–46 percent (addition and subtraction), 2 percent (multiplication and division) 4: 55–67 percent (addition and subtraction), 21–32 percent (multiplication and division) 5: 80–86 percent (addition and subtraction), 50–53 percent (multiplication and division) 6: 76–82 percent (addition and subtraction), 59–67 percent (multiplication and division)
What student data do we want to improve?	Each teacher is looking at their trends and doing an action plan Grade 1: Look at Rocket Math or Bubble Gum Math After-school mathematics intervention for referred students started approximately one month ago by intervention teachers Sixth-grade students who are not yet proficient are in a Tier 3 intervention or receiving special education services
What challenges do we face?	Behavior Data 1 suspension: possession of weapon Major referrals: 5 (1 possession of weapon, 2 fighting or physical aggression, 1 abusive language or profanity, 1 harassment or bullying) Minor referrals: 25 (8 defiance or disrespect, 2 disruption, 11 nonserious but inappropriate physical contact, 4 low-intensity inappropriate language)
What do we need to learn more about and understand better?	Meditation after lunchtime recess Lab given to students recommended by teachers for extra support approximately one month ago
Based on our assumptions, what can the team investigate today, tomorrow, or next week to confirm or contradict our assumptions and beliefs?	Are students moving out of reading intervention? Do the students identified in behavior data reflect a specific grade level?

Figure 2.1: MTSS improvement team agenda template.

By promoting and using the guiding questions of an MTSS improvement team, the team can broaden the scope of conversations to investigate larger systemic factors that may hinder student learning. These conversations might include the lack of evidence-based interventions across the school, equity of resources and supports across grades or content areas, or a particular instructional strategy's effectiveness across classrooms. These broader perspectives help build collaborative conversations and considerations about what teams need to analyze and improve.

If schools and districts are going to improve their current systems, establishing a learning-focused team that engages in continuous improvement is critical. *Continuous improvement* is research that involves multiple iterative cycles of activity over extended periods (Bryk et al., 2015). MTSS requires continuous improvement cycles of inquiry and methods, focused on learning what works best, to address the systemic challenges in meeting student learning needs. With the primary goal of learning through rapid cycles of inquiry, improvement teams gain insight into what to do and how to do it more effectively. The purpose of rapid learning cycles is to determine what works before scaling the innovation so you can later implement the change systemwide with a higher degree of confidence that will improve the specific goal. We discuss continuous improvement further in chapter 6 (page 117).

We recommend an iterative model using small, controlled learning opportunities called Plan-Do-Study-Act (PDSA; Bryk et al., 2015). This process generates data that inform the MTSS improvement team about what systematic actions it needs to improve student outcomes. The PDSA cycle is a form of action research inquiry, guiding rapid learning based on a hypothesis for improvement, allowing a team to test out an improvement action quickly, and gathering data to determine if the hypothesis is correct. This process allows organizations to start small and learn fast prior to engaging in large system change (Bryk et al., 2015; Langley et al., 2009). We discuss the PDSA model in more depth in chapter 6 (page 117).

Against the backdrop of the PLC process, MTSS improvement teams can work to build, enhance, and create the necessary collaborative leadership structures for an effective MTSS framework. This is not quick or easy to do. PLC implementation takes time and, as many educators know, can even take years to implement. MTSS improvement teams involve thinking differently. These new ideas will involve a new approach that will require thoughtful communication and messaging before setting on the path toward building an MTSS framework. While challenging, work in service of student learning is well worth it.

Communication and Messaging

Successful MTSS implementation depends on a strategic messaging approach. Building stakeholders' collective commitments to the purpose of MTSS requires school and district leadership to design a well-crafted communication and messaging plan. Messaging is about clarity and in building clarity you refine the purpose around vision and mission. A lack of clarity can take its toll on an organization's performance related to production, engagement, and communication (Martin, 2012). A clear and concise message creates the right conditions for professional learning and collective impact. This effort begins by articulating a message about why MTSS is important and what will be required of staff.

Developing the right messaging strategy takes time but is worth it. Not taking the time to craft the right message can result in missteps with communication or incorrect assumptions and beliefs that lead to stalled implementation efforts. According to management consultant Karen Martin (2012), "Unclear communication is a deeply embedded habit in most organizations" (p. 18). Often, leaders lack focus, clarity, engagement, and discipline to attend to the significance of clear communication, which begins with messaging. Clear messaging builds focus on the right priority, which helps avoid the problem of messages that communicate everything as a priority, resulting in nothing being prioritized (Martin, 2012).

When you first introduce MTSS, staff members may have questions such as the following.

- What is MTSS?

- Why do we need to build and implement an MTSS framework?

- What does it require that we are not already doing?

- How is it different from RTI?

These are just a few questions you might encounter as you build momentum for prioritizing MTSS. If you cannot answer them in a clear and compelling way, the questions can go on and on and ultimately derail communication and implementation efforts right out of the gate. You can avoid this with the right communication strategy. When crafting strategic, transparent communication and messaging for MTSS, consider the following characteristics, which we will then cover in detail.

- Engage stakeholders early on to provide perspectives on what MTSS is and is not.

- Know the stakeholders who have an interest in MTSS and what they need to know.

- Develop a clear and concise message map for implementing MTSS.

- Find the right person to deliver or open the communication (sometimes a credible messenger is more important than the message).

- Communicate clearly what the team needs to do first and how to sustain the implementation efforts.

- Prioritize learning over quick changes and solutions.

These considerations are critical to constructing a message that involves the right stakeholders, considers their insights and perspectives, and ultimately builds trust and collaboration so that MTSS becomes a team effort, not a top-down directive. As an example, to engage stakeholders early, leaders might consider pulling a team together to look at the research on MTSS. Most stakeholders and educational partners are invited into conversations after leaders have decided on the initiative. This approach can set an adversarial tone where leaders must prove to stakeholders that they made the right decision. Compare this to the approach of engaging teams in a learning journey early on, where leaders, staff, and stakeholders work together to learn what might be the best way to accomplish shared goals. Teams discover together the research and expertise about what other organizations have done to engage in MTSS. An MTSS team formed in this manner will be better equipped to clearly articulate a message to mobilize staff.

A clearly articulated message that resonates with stakeholders requires moving beyond the typical calls to action. As an example of the types of communication we often hear, consider the following.

> "We need to change the way we collaborate in order to build an MTSS framework."

This statement may resonate with some team members but may not be clear to others as to why they need to change the way they collaborate. It clearly calls for change but does not explain why. Consider the following alternative, which responds to a common traditional practice and calls for a shift to a more effective alternative.

> "There is no evidence that shaming students about their test scores improves their performance. The only thing that we know changes students' outcomes is deep collaboration around student learning needs."

This message explains that improving student learning is the reason for the change and sets the tone for a call to action. Developing a clear call to action with the right tone for your audience empowers a team and allows for clear articulation of what teams need to do and how to do it.

Once you open with a clear statement, you can organize your message by stating how you will reach the goal: the priority actions that will get you where you want to go. State no more than three priorities that define what teams will need to do. Continuing the preceding example, for instance, the leader might add the following.

> "To create the collaboration we need to improve student outcomes, we need to reinvest in our professional collaboration structures; build a continuum of tiered supports around students' academic, behavioral, and social-emotional needs; and use evidence-based and high-leverage teaching practices in our daily instruction."

This message lays out a map of what the team needs to accomplish to build the foundation of an MTSS framework. The three messages in the statement are: (1) reinvest in the team's professional collaboration structures, (2) build a continuum of supports, and (3) use evidence-based and high-leverage teaching practices. From here, you can begin to fill in how your team will accomplish these goals.

Defining how the team will get the work done is most effective with a tool called a *message map*. A message map helps create, organize, and prioritize the critical information from the opening statement. Message maps allow listeners to understand more about the direction and implementation of an initiative. Figure 2.2 shows a sample message map that can help formulate your organization's approach. A blank reproducible appears at the end of the chapter (page 36).

	Message 1	Message 2	Message 3
What	Reinvest in our professional collaboration structures.	Build a continuum of supports around students' needs.	Use evidence-based and high-leverage teaching practices.
How	Reassess our stages of collaboration.	Become experts in assessing student learning.	Investigate what evidence-based and high-leverage practices are.
How	Focus on analyzing student results.	Prioritize tiers around student learning needs.	Identify evidence-based interventions and practices that support students best.
How	Prioritize our team time to build the right relationships and communication structures.	Communicate about our site leaders' challenges and barriers to implementation.	Build collective commitments as teachers to use both evidence-based and high-leverage practices.

Source: Adapted from Smith, 2014.

Figure 2.2: Message map example.

Using a message map allows you to formulate a strategic communication plan for building an MTSS framework. Once teams have identified a clear call to action about what they want to accomplish, they can begin to brainstorm and prioritize the actions they will need to take to accomplish the goal by creating concise, clearly articulated statements of what needs to be done. The message map will help you organize your team's ideas and methods for implementation.

At this point in the messaging, selecting the right person to deliver the message can help build further credibility in the implementation plan. The messenger may or may not be the school or district leader; it might be someone considered a leader or influencer among the staff and a source of credibility and knowledge. Having the right staff member deliver the message conveys that collaboration and planning have been thoughtfully implemented by a team that understands the system's unique needs, and ultimately provides the team and the school with a clear path for action. Again, continuing our example, a school or district leader might introduce an expert and influential team member as follows.

> "To better explain how we intend to get the three areas of work done, we have asked our intervention lead to share our next steps for building an MTSS framework."

When developing an MTSS communication plan, identify the initial implementation steps and how they will impact the stakeholders receiving the message. Enacting an MTSS framework will take time. Let your stakeholders know this in advance by providing time frames or benchmarks so stakeholders can visualize the journey and understand it will progress over time. These realistic expectations generate endurance and sustainability for the work.

A final item for consideration in messaging for MTSS is the process of learning by testing different approaches to see what improves student outcomes and what does not. Help your stakeholders understand that this process may be different from what they have experienced before. For stakeholders in organizations that traditionally impose quick, unilateral changes, the MTSS process is new and will be challenging at times. However, this more collaborative approach will lead to better results.

Tools for Building Your MTSS Framework

So far in this chapter, we have underscored the importance of building collaborative leadership structures such as PLCs, MTSS improvement teams, and communication and messaging. With this foundational knowledge, teams and schools can begin the journey of developing their own MTSS framework. To help you apply the element of collaborative leadership structures in your organization, this section presents a case study, a team activity, a component audit, and an action plan.

Case Study

The following case study exemplifies an MTSS approach to establishing collaborative leadership structures for MTSS and demonstrates the preferred method for how an MTSS team would approach a problem of practice.

District MTSS Improvement Team

In Lakefront School District, the district MTSS improvement team is focused on building a strategic action plan for MTSS for the upcoming school year. The team is comprised of the superintendent, the director of special education, a district office administrator, a paraprofessional, the school psychologists, the school-home liaison, an office manager, a general education teacher, a special education teacher, a curriculum coach, the principals, and a community stakeholder. Each team member has an opportunity to analyze and discuss school-level student performance data. The team members share their views on what conclusions can be drawn, what assumptions are made, and what questions they have that need to be answered. The team categorizes the questions so that each question goes to the team member who is best equipped to investigate or answer the question. By grouping the questions and assigning specific individuals to answer those questions, the team builds collective focus on learning more and more until they can define the need and next steps more clearly.

For example, the team identifies a high number of students who are experiencing homelessness or living in foster care and need targeted Tier 2 supports. These data generate a question: "Are our homeless and foster-care students coming to school regularly?" The team assigns the investigation of that question to the principals, who will gather attendance data for those two groups of students and share at the next meeting. At the following meeting, the principals share that students experiencing homelessness or living in foster care are chronically absent from schools across the district. The team agrees that this may contribute to the need for more targeted Tier 2 supports. The MTSS team then decides to use an approach called *empathy interviews* (a set of questions that allow the questioner to better understand the problem from the interviewee's perspective) to get a clearer sense of the problems associated with the chronic absences of these students. In this case, the team determines that the school psychologists, general education teacher, and special education teacher will conduct empathy interviews with a sample of families affected by homelessness or foster care.

After the team members complete interviews with three different affected families, they compile a list of their findings and the team discusses potential changes. One of the findings was that all three families were unaware of how the students' absences were impacting their academic and behavioral needs for more intensive services. The team decided to put the families on a call list: if the students are absent, a staff member will call them immediately to find out what the school can do to either support the student coming to school or provide schoolwork and support while they are out. The team then tests this idea using a six- to eight-week PDSA cycle. The team showed that immediate calls to families improved communication between the school and the families and improved the students' attendance by 40 percent. The team logged every call and, over time, showed that each family required fewer calls and student attendance improved. The team then set out to construct a strategic plan to implement the tested idea as a districtwide practice.

This case study highlights the unique roles and functions of the district MTSS improvement team. The fundamental reason the MTSS improvement team approach is different from other approaches is because the MTSS improvement team consists of educators closest to the issues—in other words, directly affected by the problem or challenge. An improvement team is focused on learning. Executing this approach requires specific stakeholders be part of the team. Involving those closest enacts a user-centered approach to MTSS implementation and engages the team in "examining the problem from the point of view of the user—the person who is experiencing it firsthand" (Bryk et al., 2015, p. 13). If you are going to build an MTSS improvement team, include those who will be most affected by the changes, initiatives, and implementation of MTSS.

Answer the following questions about the case study and discuss them with your team. See page 37 for a reproducible version of these questions.

- What did you notice or learn from the case study?

- How does the case study exemplify the core components of this chapter?

- How do the team's actions in the case study serve the goal of ensuring all students learn?

Team Activity

The team activity allows you to reflect on what you have read in this chapter and apply it with your team. It is an opportunity to assess your organization's current state and decide the best next steps for building the collaborative leadership structures of your MTSS framework. Each member should answer the questions in the team activity individually and then share responses with the team. See page 38 for a reproducible version of this activity.

- What portion of the chapter resonated with you most?

- What is your organization's current reality when it comes to collaborative leadership?

- What do you think needs to change in your organization?

- What effective practices do you think need to continue in your organization?

- What steps do you suggest your organization take to improve collaborative leadership?

Component Audit

The component audit for collaborative leadership guides you to assess the most essential elements to build a strong foundation for the work ahead. After learning about professional collaboration, MTSS improvement teams, and communication and messaging in this chapter, use the following steps to complete the component audit with your teams.

1. Have team members independently score the implementation status of each of the listed components in your school or district.

2. Compare scores within the team.

3. Discuss with your team to determine which component will be the most effective starting point—which one will have the biggest impact right now?

Figure 2.3 displays the component audit for collaborative leadership. See page 39 for a reproducible version of this component audit.

Component	Essential Elements	Status
Professional Collaboration Systemwide, learning-focused collaboration, such as the professional learning community process, is taking place.	• Collaborative teams are fully in place for each content or grade level and have operating norms and agendas aligned to the four critical questions of a PLC. • Collaborative teams develop common assessments, know what students have learned, and what proficiency looks like.	☐ Not yet implemented ☐ Partially implemented ☐ Fully implemented ☐ Sustaining implementation
	• Collaborative teams analyze student learning results and adjust instruction as needed based on specific learning targets. • Collaborative teams adapt instruction by using universally accessible instruction that meets various student learning needs. • Collaborative teams reflect on instructional challenges and have a feedback loop with site leadership teams to identify trends, challenges, and opportunities with instruction.	
MTSS Improvement Teams MTSS improvement teams guide MTSS framework development.	• MTSS improvement teams have established feedback loops with PLCs regarding student performance data. • MTSS improvement teams regularly review progress on the MTSS framework.	☐ Not yet implemented ☐ Partially implemented ☐ Fully implemented ☐ Sustaining implementation
Communication and Messaging Teams understand the purpose of MTSS and have clearly communicated the goals and how they will achieve those goals.	• Teams and stakeholders are included in the process and understand the purpose of building an MTSS framework. • Communication and messaging include the importance and integration of all site and district leadership teams. • Teams understand the goals of MTSS and can articulate how they will accomplish the goals.	☐ Not yet implemented ☐ Partially implemented ☐ Fully implemented ☐ Sustaining implementation

Figure 2.3: MTSS component audit—Collaborative leadership.

Action Plan

Based on the results of your team activity and component audit, develop your action plan for implementing collaborative leadership structures, as exemplified in figure 2.4 (page 34). A reproducible action plan appears on page 40. In this sample, the team selected professional collaboration as the component that their component audit indicates is the most effective starting point. To improve their status on this component, their action plan defines steps they can take for each element that makes up professional collaboration.

Beginning date:	Collaborative Leadership	Check when completed
_____	**Component:** Professional collaboration (systemwide, learning-focused collaboration, such as the PLC process, is taking place)	
Action plan	Ensure grade-level and content-area collaborative teams have operating norms and agendas aligned to the four critical questions of a PLC. The principal and grade-level chairs will meet to determine expectations and create sample norms and agendas.	
	Build on existing knowledge about developing common assessments, knowing what students have learned, and ascertaining what proficiency looks like. Grade-level teams will focus on developing at least one common assessment for the next units of instruction.	
	Analyze student learning results and adjust instruction as needed based on specific learning targets. Grade-level teams will meet to determine how best to have this discussion at least monthly.	
	Develop teachers' capacity to adapt instruction by using universally accessible instruction that meets various student learning needs. The principal will work with the district to determine professional learning around universal instructional strategies.	
	Create communication channels between collaborative teams and site leadership team to identify trends, challenges, and opportunities with instruction. The site leadership team will meet to determine how best to coordinate communication with grade-level teams.	
How will you monitor the implementation? What evidence will you examine?	• Review progress updates on each action step at regular meetings. • Plan for professional learning and communication. • Create and review artifacts such as norms, agendas, and common assessments.	

Figure 2.4: Sample action plan for MTSS implementation—Collaborative leadership.

Summary

This chapter explores the essential components of collaborative leadership within an MTSS framework: professional collaboration, MTSS improvement teams, and communication and messaging. We provide key information about each component and provide information on how to get started in your organization. The journey of improving collaborative leadership structures in your school or district is most likely long and complicated, so the need for coordinated efforts is significant. As a result, we recommend that you give profound thought and consideration to a plan that focuses on building PLCs, using an MTSS improvement team, and applying strategic communication and messaging. In the next chapter, we address universal access.

MTSS Improvement Team Agenda

Agenda Questions	Agenda Discussion Notes
What do the data tell us currently?	
What student data do we want to improve?	
What challenges do we face?	
What do we need to learn more about and understand better?	
Based on our assumptions, what can the team investigate today, tomorrow, or next week to confirm or contradict our assumptions and beliefs?	

Demystifying MTSS © 2023 Solution Tree Press • SolutionTree.com

Visit **go.SolutionTree.com/schoolimprovement** to download this free reproducible.

Message Map

To support the primary message of implementing MTSS to help all students learn, identify three key messages. For each of the three messages, identify the *what*—the specific statement of action. Then identify *how* your team will complete that action.

	Message 1	**Message 2**	**Message 3**
What			
How			
How			
How			

Source: Adapted from Smith, A. (2014, April). Stuart leadership meeting workshop 5 *[Conference presentation]. Stuart Foundation California Leaders in Education (SCALE), Los Angeles, CA.*

Chapter 2 Case Study Discussion Questions

Answer the following questions about the case study in chapter 2 (page 30) and discuss them with your team.

- What did you notice or learn from the case study?

- How does the case study exemplify the core components of this chapter?

- How do the team's actions in the case study serve the goal of ensuring all students learn?

Chapter 2 Team Activity

The team activity allows you to reflect on what you have read in chapter 2 and apply it with your team. It is an opportunity to assess your organization's current state and decide the best next steps for building the collaborative leadership structures of your MTSS framework. Each member should answer the questions in the team activity individually and then share responses with the team.

- What portion of the chapter resonated with you most?

- What is your organization's current reality when it comes to collaborative leadership?

- What do you think needs to change in your organization?

- What effective practices do you think need to continue in your organization?

- What steps do you suggest your organization take to improve collaborative leadership?

Chapter 2 Component Audit: Collaborative Leadership

To establish your current status with the collaborative leadership part of the MTSS framework, complete the following audit.

1. Have team members independently score the implementation status of each of the identified components in your school or district.

2. Compare scores within the team.

3. Discuss with your team to determine which component will be the most effective starting point—which one will have the biggest impact right now?

Component	Essential Elements	Status
Professional Collaboration Systemwide, learning-focused collaboration, such as the professional learning community process, is taking place.	• Collaborative teams are fully in place for each content or grade level and have operating norms and agendas aligned to the four critical questions of a PLC. • Collaborative teams develop common assessments, know what students have learned, and what proficiency looks like. • Collaborative teams analyze student learning results and adjust instruction as needed based on specific learning targets. • Collaborative teams adapt instruction by using universally accessible instruction that meets various student learning needs. • Collaborative teams reflect on instructional challenges and have a feedback loop with site leadership teams to identify trends, challenges, and opportunities with instruction.	☐ Not yet implemented ☐ Partially implemented ☐ Fully implemented ☐ Sustaining implementation
MTSS Improvement Teams MTSS improvement teams guide MTSS framework development.	• MTSS improvement teams have established feedback loops with PLCs regarding student performance data. • MTSS improvement teams regularly review progress on the MTSS framework.	☐ Not yet implemented ☐ Partially implemented ☐ Fully implemented ☐ Sustaining implementation
Communication and Messaging Teams understand the purpose of MTSS and have clearly communicated the goals and how they will achieve those goals.	• Teams and stakeholders are included in the process and understand the purpose of building an MTSS framework. • Communication and messaging include the importance and integration of all site and district leadership teams. • Teams understand the goals of MTSS and can articulate how they will accomplish the goals.	☐ Not yet implemented ☐ Partially implemented ☐ Fully implemented ☐ Sustaining implementation

Demystifying MTSS © 2023 Solution Tree Press • SolutionTree.com

Visit **go.SolutionTree.com/schoolimprovement** to download this free reproducible.

Chapter 2 Action Plan for MTSS Implementation: Collaborative Leadership

Based on the results of your team activity and component audit, develop your action plan for implementing collaborative leadership. Fill in the component of collaborative leadership that you have selected as your focus. Then, list tangible actions that will help improve the status of this component in your school or district, perhaps using the essential elements listed in the component audit as a guide. Finally, define the evidence that you will use to monitor your progress. This action-plan template will build through each chapter into a strategic plan to set the course for long-term implementation.

Beginning date: _____	Collaborative Leadership Component:	Check when completed
Action plan		
How will you monitor the implementation? What evidence will you examine?		

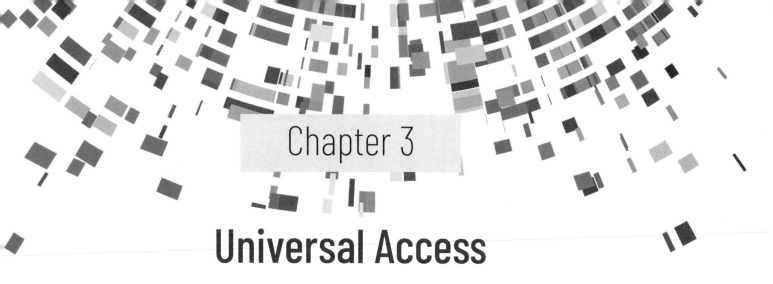

Chapter 3

Universal Access

In order to support all students, an MTSS framework must make high-quality academic instruction and behavioral and social-emotional supports available to all students. This is what it means to provide universal access. The key to a strong MTSS framework is a core instructional model that accounts for the variability of learners in a classroom and a system that allows all students access to supplementary supports when they need them. Organizations can design and implement such access to prevent students from falling behind. As we have discussed in prior chapters, MTSS is a proactive approach. In this chapter, we describe high-quality inclusive instruction, including our preferred model, Universal Design for Learning, and detail how educators should administer screeners, provide supports, and monitor progress for all students.

Inclusive Instruction

Inclusive instruction begins with educators' belief that they are responsible for improving outcomes for all students, including students historically underserved in the traditional education system. These students, including students with disabilities, students who receive special education services, multilanguage learners, and other underserved student groups, have great potential to benefit from universal instruction. Inclusive instruction honors all students with their own unique backgrounds, strengths, and challenges by proactively creating lessons and learning environments that maximize their strengths while removing barriers to their success. As mentioned previously, our preferred model for inclusive instruction is UDL, which we describe in the following sections.

What Is UDL?

Universal Design for Learning is a method anchored in best practices and research that helps build a high-quality, accessible instructional framework. These pedagogical principles guide educator planning and delivery of universally accessible learning targets and skills (Meyer, Rose, & Gordon, 2014). The Center for Applied Special Technology (CAST, 2018), the nonprofit education research and development organization that created UDL, further defines UDL as "a framework to improve and optimize teaching and learning for all people based on scientific insights into how humans learn." Other sources describe UDL as follows.

- "A best-practice approach in Tier 1 classroom design for instruction. It takes into consideration the variability in learning, so lessons are designed with this in mind" (Hannigan & Hannigan, 2021, p. 9).

- "A blueprint for creating instructional goals, methods, materials, and assessments that work for everyone—not a single, one-size-fits-all solution but rather flexible approaches that can be customized and adjusted for individual needs" (UDL on Campus, n.d.).

- "An instructional framework that educators can use as they plan curriculum and instruction. UDL guidelines can be applied to the designing of instructional goals, methods, materials, and assessment to build in flexible paths for learning" (Rao et al., 2017, p. 37).

In lessons designed with UDL, the learning goal is the same for all students, and each student can reach that goal in a variety of ways. UDL enhances teachers' practice, builds their knowledge and capacity, and reduces the tensions a system may experience when taking on the challenge of building universal access and supports as part of the MTSS framework.

The UDL framework is based on neuroscientific research that identifies brain structures engaged in the learning process (Meyer et al., 2014). These structures provide the groundwork for the three foundational principles of UDL, designed to provide equity and access to rigorous learning standards for all students.

1. Provide multiple means of engagement

2. Provide multiple means of representation

3. Provide multiple means of action and expression (Meyer et al., 2014, p. 7)

Through these three principles, UDL recognizes the diversity and variability of learners. UDL accommodates students' natural variability by intentionally designing learning opportunities and environments that increase accessibility (Coyne et al., 2017). Once they recognize that they can proactively design lessons that are accessible for all students, teachers no longer use a one-size-fits-all approach to instruction. Instead, UDL instruction engages more students with the content, accessing rigorous grade-level standards, thereby decreasing the number of students requiring more intensive supports in their education. When teachers intentionally design lessons based on UDL, they proactively engage students, make the learning relevant, and create multiple means to deliver content. UDL also provides students with opportunities to demonstrate knowledge and understanding in their unique ways (Navarro, Zervas, Gesa, & Sampson, 2016). Further, this engagement results in fewer problematic behaviors that teachers need to address in the classroom. When lessons provide various ways to access content, engage learners, and allow them to demonstrate their learning in different ways, negative behaviors and behaviors to escape the learning environment decrease (Shafritz, Ott, & Jang, 2016).

It is essential to understand that UDL does not apply solely to unique and vulnerable subgroups such as special education. Unfortunately, this is a common misperception. As suggested by its name, UDL applies *universally* to all students. It is a scientifically based framework that guides all aspects of the learning environment (Nelson & Basham, 2014) and, as part of the MTSS framework for a school or district, helps strengthen instructional Tier 1 practices and instruction for all students. Lessons that minimize barriers to learning are critical for dual language and neurodiverse students, yes, but teachers who are successful with UDL use the principles to design lessons and assessments that are inherently accessible to each and every student.

Why UDL?

So *why* is UDL an essential element for building your MTSS framework? The answer is that UDL is good for all learners and is recommended by multiple education policies. Each of the educational policies listed in table 3.1 identifies UDL as an effective educational framework that teachers can use to achieve equity and access for all students (Williams, 2020).

Table 3.1: UDL in Education Policy

Legislation	Summary	Inclusion of UDL
Individuals With Disabilities Act (IDEA, 2004)	IDEA outlines services and protections for students identified with a qualifying disability.	IDEA recommends universal design principles for increasing access to general-education curriculum for students with disabilities.
Higher Education Opportunity Act (2008)	This act outlines new requirements for institutions and offers grants for college programs and students, lowering college costs, safety plans, and loans.	The Higher Education Opportunity Act features UDL as a means for greater access.
Every Student Succeeds Act (ESSA, 2015)	ESSA is the reauthorization of the Elementary and Secondary Education Act from 1965 and creates a focus on preparing students for success in college and careers.	• ESSA explicitly focuses on equity and requires academic rigor to prepare for college and career. • This act calls for information on student progress to be made public. • This act also requires using UDL principles to make assessment systems accessible to all students.

continued →

Legislation	Summary	Inclusion of UDL
National Education Technology Plan (Office of Educational Technology, 2017)	This act sets a national vision and plan for learning technology and identifies key examples and activities for the effective use of technology and accessibility to technology in a meaningful way.	• The National Education Technology Plan focuses on equity and access. • This act identifies an infrastructure to support all-the-time, everywhere learning. • It also elevates UDL as the foundation for accessible design.
Ontario Human Rights Code (Ontario Human Rights Commission, 2018)	Ontario's Human Rights Code and associated policies require accessible educational services for all students, including students with disabilities.	The Ontario Human Rights Code cites UDL for its emphasis on inclusive participation, taking down barriers, flexibility, and high expectations for all.

There's little debate that UDL is one of the most promising ways to equip students for success. As educational practitioners, we all aspire to build great systems to meet students' learning needs. To do this, you need a standardized process. As district leaders and UDL experts Katie Novak and Kristan Rodriguez (2016) state, "We need a process based on research and best-practice . . . that allows us to monitor our long-term success, so the process is personalized for our very unique landscape. UDL allows us to do just that" (p. viii).

How Do We Implement UDL?

How willing and committed are your staff to building a high-quality Tier 1 instructional framework that can meet the needs of all learners? What is your staff's current ability to build that high-quality Tier 1 instructional framework? In most school systems, these two questions have very different answers. In most cases, educational practitioners desire to deliver a high-quality instructional framework that meets the needs of all learners. The core of the problem is educators lack the ability and knowledge to implement the framework. Building a high-quality Tier 1 framework anchored in best practices and research is no easy feat. It typically requires extensive, ongoing professional learning and may create anxiety, stress, and frustration for educators as they begin building cohesive schoolwide or districtwide expectations. Building a high-quality instructional framework for your school or district takes time. However, in our experience, three steps are essential to getting started in implementing the UDL principles of multiple means of engagement, representation, and action and expression.

The first step is to explore and review what UDL is. Giving teams the opportunity to explore and review the research behind UDL is critical, as is establishing the structures and systems in which teams can learn about and understand UDL principles. For example, school leaders could set aside protected time during the workday to explore research related to UDL. This time for exploration and review helps build understanding and encourages educators to think about the framework as a beneficial endeavor. It also gives rise to productive questions, such as, Where has UDL been successful? What does student performance look like in places where UDL is implemented? Can I watch a UDL lesson and compare it to my own? All these questions set up the next step.

The second step is to investigate. As teams explore and review the UDL principles and research, they begin to ask more questions. This step allows teams to investigate UDL's effectiveness and what UDL looks like in practice. We recommend the following resources for investigating UDL.

- CAST (www.cast.org)

- Universal Design for Learning Implementation and Research Network (https://udl-irn.org/about)

- The UDL Project (www.theudlproject.com)

It's important in this phase that teams do not view UDL as a silver-bullet idea or a flavor-of-the-month initiative. As teams will discover, UDL implementation is a long-term commitment that will ensure success for all students (Novak & Rodriguez, 2016).

The third step is to design and implement. After teams have explored UDL principles and investigated the fundamental design principles associated with UDL, give them permission to design and implement lessons that employ the UDL principles. We recommend allowing teachers to start with one principle at a time and to choose which principle they experiment with first (noting that giving educators a choice on where to begin is not the same as giving them a choice on whether or not to begin; Novak & Rodriguez, 2016). Designing lessons that integrate one of the three principles of UDL moves the process forward, helps educators build knowledge around how to anticipate students' learning needs, and creates in-depth learning opportunities for teachers and students. Table 3.2 lists ways teachers can begin applying the three principles.

The goal of inclusive instruction and UDL in particular is to provide the broadest access to learning for all students during initial instruction. The three-step approach to building educators' knowledge of and ability to design learning experiences strengthens the quality of teaching and learning in Tier 1. However, a high-quality instructional framework doesn't stop with Tier 1. It requires that teacher teams understand the relationship between Tier 1 and Tiers 2 and 3. In the next section, we describe how universal monitoring in Tier 1 leads into the more targeted supports in Tiers 2 and 3.

Table 3.2: Applying the UDL Principles

Provide Multiple Means of Engagement	Provide Multiple Means of Representation	Provide Multiple Means of Action and Expression
Generating Interest • Optimize individual choice and autonomy. • Optimize relevance, value, and authenticity. • Minimize threats and distractions.	**Communicating Information** • Offer ways of customizing the display of information. • Offer alternatives for auditory information. • Offer alternatives for visual information.	**Using Physical Action** • Vary the methods students can use to process and present their learning. • Optimize access to tools and assistive technologies.

continued →

Provide Multiple Means of Engagement	Provide Multiple Means of Representation	Provide Multiple Means of Action and Expression
Sustaining Effort and Persistence • Ensure learners clearly understand and can see goals and objectives. • Optimize the level of challenge for students by adjusting the level of rigor and allowing students varying degrees of scaffold supports (such as mind maps, sentence frames, and anchor charts). • Foster collaboration and community. • Increase mastery-oriented feedback.	**Clarifying Language and Symbols** • Clarify vocabulary and symbols. • Clarify syntax and structure. • Support decoding of text, mathematical notation, and symbols. • Provide translation tools, supply links to definitions, and support language with pictures or images. • Illustrate ideas through multiple media.	**Supporting Expression and Communication** • Use multiple media for communication. • Use multiple tools for construction and composition, such as talk-to-text software, manipulatives, and sentence starters. • Offer scaffolds so students can access the learning while increasing fluency as they work toward mastery.
Promoting Self-Regulation • Promote expectations and beliefs that optimize motivation. • Facilitate personal coping skills and strategies. • Develop self-assessment and reflection.	**Supporting Comprehension** • Activate or supply background knowledge. • Highlight patterns, critical features, big ideas, and relationships. • Guide information processing and visualization. • Ensure students can apply their learning to various content and contexts.	**Facilitating Executive Function** • Guide appropriate goal setting. • Support planning and strategy development. • Facilitate managing information and resources. • Guide students to set goals and monitor their own progress and understanding.

Source: Adapted from CAST, 2018.

Universal Monitoring

MTSS requires a comprehensive view of data to improve outcomes. This includes collecting data on all students to monitor progress and identify needs. The U.S. Department of Education (2017) states:

> A multi-tiered system of support is a framework designed to respond to the needs of all students within a system which integrates, but is not limited to, tiered behavior supports (e.g. positive behavior interventions and supports [PBIS]) and academic (e.g. Response to Intervention—RTI) supports. MTSS is a whole-school, data-driven, prevention-based framework for improving student learning outcomes for all students through a layered continuum of evidence-based practices and systems.

In order to support students academically and behaviorally at all three tiers, your MTSS framework must provide universal support as part of Tier 1 and collect information to determine which students need additional support. In the following sections, we describe data-based practices that apply to all students: universal screeners, universal supports, and universal progress monitoring.

Universal Screeners

Screening tools produce data to identify students who may need additional supports to be successful (McIntosh & Goodman, 2016). Academic, behavioral, and social-emotional screeners provide critical information about each student's baseline status and ongoing learning. Universal screening is a process of gathering academic and behavior data about all the students in a class, grade, school, or district to identify which students may need additional assistance to meet learning goals (Brown-Chidsey & Bickford, 2016). For example, suppose a high school wants to screen its students for basic mathematics skills. They might produce or purchase a screener to give all incoming freshmen to assess their current mathematics skills. This assessment provides the mathematics department detailed information about students' readiness. It also helps the site leadership determine placement in courses that will best remediate or accelerate students' acquisition of necessary skills to enable them to be more successful.

Universal screeners come in different formats from electronic platform assessments to direct teacher assessment. Academic universal screeners are designed to be short in duration, since they are usually aimed at identifying a student's accuracy and fluency in relationship to a specific essential skill or standard. Curriculum-based measurement (CBM) and Dynamic Indicators of Basic Early Literacy Skills (DIBELS) are examples of academic screeners (Hughes & Dexter, n.d.). For universal screening of behavior, a school's or district's office discipline referrals can serve by standardizing the process, training, forms, and definitions of behaviors. Schools can also purchase behavioral and social-emotional screeners such as the BASC-3 Behavioral and Emotional Screening System (Kamphaus & Reynolds, 2015).

While teams can and will still use their own assessments to identify student needs, universal screeners provide more accurate and efficient metrics that allow educators to respond. They provide consistent data that educators can use and compare, both between students or groups of students and for progress monitoring of individual students. Cut points or guidelines about how students score on screeners also allow educators to prioritize students who show risk factors and consequently determine if they require tiered support and resources (Allain & Eberhardt, 2011; McIntosh & Goodman, 2016).

Universal screeners can also provide formative data in a timely manner. Frequently, districts find themselves using summative data (such as state test scores) from the prior year or waiting for classroom assessment data to accumulate, delaying the time in which students could have been receiving intervention and supports. The power of universal screening tools in Tier 1 is the early identification of students at risk for academic failure or behavioral deregulation. This approach enables a level of prevention for all students by improving educators' ability to identify students' needs and respond promptly with universal supports or targeted interventions.

The data that universal screeners provide also supply insight into the strengths and weaknesses of the framework itself. If many students are performing below expectations on a certain academic screener, that is evidence that Tier 1 instruction needs improvement. For example, if a disproportionate number of second-grade students fall behind grade-level reading expectations and the data from universal screeners indicate a deficit in phonemic awareness, this may be indicative of a problem in Tier 1 instruction or a need to improve the curriculum. It will be more effective and efficient to allocate resources to teacher training or purchase curriculum materials that support effective instruction in phonics than to refer a large number of students to Tier 2 or Tier 3 support. As a behavioral example, data may indicate a large number of altercations when students are waiting for the bus after school. Leaders could bolster Tier 1 systems by increasing the supervision at this time in this location, modeling and teaching schoolwide safety behaviors and so on, rather than spending resources on more intensive responses.

Universal Supports

Once educators can identify student needs using universal screeners, they can then determine how best to support them. Tier 1 support is preventative and available to all students. An academic example would be a small-group reteach for students who did not grasp a concept during a lesson. To support behavior in Tier 1, teachers would explicitly teach the behavior expectations for different locations of the school—for example, walking in the halls, keeping voices low in the library, and taking turns on the playground. Tier 2 and Tier 3 interventions are also universal in the sense that they are available to all students as needed. If screeners indicate a student has unmet academic or behavioral needs, that student would immediately receive services in addition to Tier 1 instruction. Universal supports allow a team to take preventative measures and target resources and assistance to students who are most in need.

Making supports accessible to all students can reduce the likelihood of what coauthor Matt's former assistant superintendent Rich Smith often referred to as SST, or *supersonic transport* to special education. In other words, systems that lack high-quality universal instruction and supports often over-identify students for special education or do so without first attempting less disruptive methods. Universal supports give all students access without the penalty of missing core instruction and must look very different from traditional instructional strategies. Examples of universal supports in Tier 1 are as follows.

- Intensify the frequency of in-class supports and interventions.
- Increase the duration of time devoted to building a skill.
- Create smaller groups of students to accelerate and remediate.
- Create a variety of ways for students to demonstrate understanding of content.
- Build a student-centered master schedule.
- Establish student check-in and check-out meetings.

- Use PBIS.

- Use culturally responsive teaching practices.

- Use restorative justice practices.

- Incorporate character education programs.

- Use trauma-informed practices.

Measures such as these prevent most students from requiring more intensive (that is, Tier 2 or Tier 3) supports and interventions.

The key takeaway here is that universal supports mean everyone has access. If you are designing supports in ways that limit the team's ability to implement them or limit access for students, then they are not universal. We often see this in schools when students who require supports cannot participate in other cocurricular experiences, such as band, choir, or drama. When some students go to theater or music, others receive academic support or behavioral intervention, limiting their participation in important activities. The idea that a student who requires additional support can only obtain that support by sacrificing other precious opportunities is a systemic flaw. Supports that are universally accessible for all students will require training, consultation, and innovative thinking. Do not rush to put new practices in place; invest in ensuring that teachers fully understand the nature of universal supports and why they are required (Brown-Chidsey & Bickford, 2016). As you develop your MTSS framework, the key is not to segregate students into tiers but to prioritize Tier 1. When building Tier 1 systems, prioritize the term *universal* in all that you do.

Universal Progress Monitoring

Progress monitoring is the only way to know if a practice or support is working. Effective progress monitoring allows educators and teams to determine if students are responding to classroom and systemwide interventions and supports over time. Universal progress-monitoring tools must capture the effectiveness of Tier 1 instruction and support for all students. Progress monitoring for students' academic, behavioral, or social-emotional needs allows educators to access data about student progress.

Universal progress monitoring should be conducted at coordinated times at a regular frequency. In Tier 1, all students are assessed on a benchmark schedule, often two or three times per year. Simultaneously, universal progress monitoring provides data that help determine if more students need Tier 2 or Tier 3 supports. These data inform leaders about individual students and about the program as a whole. McIntosh and Goodman (2016) make this clear: "if a significant portion (e.g., over 20%) of students need support beyond Tier 1 to achieve academic and behavioral goals, then the Tier 1 program is not sufficient as implemented" (p. 60).

The frequency of progress monitoring increases in each tier. Universal progress-monitoring data for Tier 1 are complemented with more frequent checks for Tier 2 and Tier 3. These data represent key indicators that help students get timely access to academic, behavioral, and social-emotional instruction and support they need when they need it (McCart & Miller, 2020). This means that progress monitoring must be frequent and efficient—*not* such a daunting task that a great deal of instructional time passes before teachers receive and are able to act on the data.

The key is to integrate progress monitoring into Tier 1 to create a foundation for more intense and specific monitoring in the higher tiers. Some questions to guide your decisions about monitoring progress are as follows.

- How would we use data to guide our next steps, and how would we do this for all students?

- What does the universal screener indicate students need?

- What are the learning goals (academic, behavioral, and social-emotional)?

- What progress-monitoring tools (curriculum-based tools, teacher observation, and school- or districtwide assessments) do we have access to?

- Who (teachers, instructional specialists, classified staff, school administrators, special education specialists) can monitor most effectively and efficiently?

- What does additional support look like for students whose monitoring indicates that what we are doing is not working?

- When do we progress monitor and how often?

When educators take these guiding factors into consideration, universal progress monitoring ensures strong instructional practices occur in Tier 1, preventing an overload of students requiring Tier 2 and 3 support. This practice also prevents teams from needing to dedicate excessive time, resources, and energy to Tier 2 and Tier 3 (McIntosh & Goodman, 2016).

Tools for Building Your MTSS Framework

So far in this chapter, we have discussed the essential components of inclusive instruction and universal monitoring. With this foundational knowledge, teams and schools can begin the journey of developing their own MTSS framework. To help you apply the element of universal access in your organization, this section presents a case study, a team activity, a component audit, and an action plan.

Case Study

The following case study exemplifies one approach to universal access in MTSS.

Universal Design for Learning

Principal Blue was eager to implement UDL as part of the Tier 1 foundation of her high school's MTSS framework but needed some way to bridge the gap between the district's initiative and her staff's reluctance to invest time and energy into another district endeavor that didn't seem like it would work for them. She asked for volunteers who would be willing to review, investigate, and design lessons using UDL. Her only requirement for the volunteer early adopters was that they learn about UDL, implement it, and share with the rest of the staff how it was working or not working. After some questions from several departments, the world history department shared that they were interested in trying UDL. The department identified a problem with the amount of reading required of students in combination with the skill gaps of literacy that made the content challenging.

They had a lengthy unit on Greek and Roman history coming up and they knew many of the students did not have pre-existing interest in the topic and some would struggle with the length of the readings. To address this problem, the team designed learning experiences that elevated the UDL principles of engagement and representation. To engage students in the topic, the teachers provided a list of topics related to Greek and Roman history that students could explore through different activities that met the standards that students were expected to learn within the unit. This gave students choice and autonomy with the topics they pursued. In addition, one of the expected readings in the unit was related to Julius Caesar. The teachers each took on the responsibility to find different versions of the reading. They had the traditional text from their adopted curriculum; one teacher found a graphic novel on Caesar and another found novels about Caesar written at various Lexile levels. By providing the various access points to engage in the topic, the teachers reported they and their students had a better experience with this unit. And student performance on assessments improved.

From this success, the department's excitement and energy were contagious. Before long, other departments at Principal Blue's high school were looking to the world history department to help rethink UDL design and implementation. Other departments stepped up to try UDL principles and before long Principal Blue had UDL spreading across her school. "It just takes one teacher, one department, one student to see UDL and the opportunities it creates for teaching and learning," Principal Blue stated at a principals' meeting. Three years later, her school has successfully closed the chasm between vision and implementation.

This case study highlights how implementing new initiatives such as UDL can start small and lead to big changes. Principal Blue, rather than focusing on mandatory implementation of UDL, focused on volunteers who were willing to try something new in hopes of addressing the learning challenges many of their students were facing. Principal Blue's patience and willingness to approach UDL with a learning mindset led to big schoolwide changes.

Answer the following questions about the case study and discuss them with your team. See page 55 for a reproducible version of these questions.

- What did you notice or learn from the case study?
- How does the case study exemplify the core components of this chapter?
- How do the team's actions in the case study serve the goal of ensuring all students learn?

Team Activity

The team activity allows you to reflect on what you have read and apply your team's learning. It is an opportunity to assess your organization's current state and decide the best next steps for building the universal access element of your MTSS framework. Each member should answer the questions in the team activity individually and then share responses with the team. See page 56 for a reproducible version of this activity.

- What portion of the chapter resonated with you most?
- What is your organization's current reality when it comes to universal access?
- What do you think needs to change in your organization?
- What effective practices do you think need to continue in your organization?
- What steps do you suggest your organization take to improve universal access?

Component Audit

The component audit for universal access guides you to assess the most essential elements to build a strong foundation for the work ahead. After reading this chapter to learn about inclusive instruction and universal monitoring, use the following steps to complete the component audit with your teams.

1. Have team members independently score the implementation status of each of the listed components in your school or district.

2. Compare scores within the team.

3. Discuss with your team to determine which component will be the most effective starting point—which one will have the biggest impact right now?

Figure 3.1 displays the component audit for universal access. See page 57 for a reproducible version of this component audit.

Component	Essential Elements	Status
Inclusive Instruction Educators understand and apply UDL principles to create high-quality core instruction.	• Teacher teams collaboratively plan fully developed UDL lessons and evaluate learning results together. • There is system-level engagement with UDL, providing teams time to review, investigate, and implement UDL principles. • UDL is reflected in academic, behavioral, and social-emotional instruction.	☐ Not yet implemented ☐ Partially implemented ☐ Fully implemented ☐ Sustaining implementation
Universal Supports, Screening, and Monitoring Educators screen and monitor all students to determine their academic and behavioral needs.	• Teacher teams have universal screeners for determining tiered support needs. • Teacher teams understand the purpose of screeners, progress monitoring, and universal and tiered supports.	☐ Not yet implemented ☐ Partially implemented ☐ Fully implemented ☐ Sustaining implementation

Figure 3.1: MTSS component audit—Universal access.

Action Plan

Based on the results of your team activity and component audit, develop your action plan for implementing universal access, as exemplified in figure 3.2. A reproducible version appears on page 58. In this sample, a team has decided to focus on screening and monitoring. They have added two action steps to improve their status and created a plan for monitoring progress.

Beginning date: _____	**Universal Access** **Component:** Universal supports, screening, and monitoring (educators screen and monitor all students to determine their academic and behavioral needs)	**Check when completed**
Action plan	Acquire universal screeners for determining tiered support needs.	
	Compile a list of options and review universal screeners for literacy and mathematics.	
	Develop teachers' understanding of the purpose of screeners, progress monitoring, and universal and tiered supports.	
	Acquire research-based resources.	
	Set aside staff meeting time to share these resources with staff and investigate the purpose of screeners.	
How will you monitor the implementation? What evidence will you examine?	• Create task forces for each action step with a leader and a group of staff who will work toward training the rest of the staff. • Share progress monthly at the site leadership team meeting.	

Figure 3.2: Sample action plan for MTSS implementation—Universal access.

Summary

This chapter details the essential elements of universal access within an MTSS framework: inclusive instruction and universal monitoring. We described UDL, the model we recommend for enacting inclusive instruction, as a way to provide high-quality Tier 1 instruction for all students. Universal monitoring, including screeners, supports, and progress monitoring, allows educators to quickly identify students whose needs are not being met by core instruction and provide supplementary supports. In the next chapter, we provide more detail about those supports at each of the three tiers.

Chapter 3 Case Study Discussion Questions

Answer the following questions about the case study in chapter 3 (page 50) and discuss them with your team.

- What did you notice or learn from the case study?

- How does the case study exemplify the core components of this chapter?

- How do the team's actions in the case study serve the goal of ensuring all students learn?

Chapter 3 Team Activity: Universal Access

The team activity allows you to reflect on what you have read in chapter 3 and apply your team's learning. It is an opportunity to assess your organization's current state and decide the best next steps for building the universal access element of your MTSS framework. Each member should answer the questions in the team activity individually and then share responses with the team.

- What portion of the chapter resonated with you most?

- What is your organization's current reality when it comes to universal access?

- What do you think needs to change in your organization?

- What effective practices do you think need to continue in your organization?

- What steps do you suggest your organization take to improve universal access?

Chapter 3 Component Audit: Universal Access

To establish your current status with the universal access part of the MTSS framework, complete the following audit.

1. Have team members independently score the implementation status of each of the identified components in your school or district.

2. Compare scores within the team.

3. Discuss with your team to determine which component will be the most effective starting point—which one will have the biggest impact right now?

Component	Essential Elements	Status
Inclusive Instruction Educators understand and apply UDL principles to create high-quality core instruction.	• Teacher teams collaboratively plan fully developed UDL lessons and evaluate learning results together. • There is system-level engagement with UDL, providing teams time to review, investigate, and implement UDL principles. • UDL is reflected in academic, behavioral, and social-emotional instruction.	☐ Not yet implemented ☐ Partially implemented ☐ Fully implemented ☐ Sustaining implementation
Universal Supports, Screening, and Monitoring Educators screen and monitor all students to determine their academic and behavioral needs.	• Teacher teams have universal screeners for determining tiered support needs. • Teacher teams understand the purpose of screeners, progress monitoring, and universal and tiered supports.	☐ Not yet implemented ☐ Partially implemented ☐ Fully implemented ☐ Sustaining implementation

Chapter 3 Action Plan for MTSS Implementation: Universal Access

Based on the results of your team activity and component audit, develop your action plan for implementing universal access. Fill in the component of universal access that you have selected as your focus. Then, list tangible actions that will help improve the status of this component in your school or district, perhaps using the essential elements listed in the component audit as a guide. Finally, define the evidence that you will use to monitor your progress. This action-plan template will build through each chapter into a strategic plan to set the course for long-term implementation.

Beginning date: _____	Universal Access Component:	Check when completed
Action plan		
How will you monitor the implementation? What evidence will you examine?		

A Continuum of Tiered Supports

In the introduction, we defined MTSS as a holistic framework that includes collaborative leadership, universal access, a continuum of tiered support systems, and data-based decision making. This chapter focuses on the element of a continuum of tiered supports, which includes the components of providing academic, behavioral, and social-emotional supports; aligning tiered resources; and using evidence-based practices. A continuum of tiered supports builds on universal access by allowing students who need additional support to receive academic, behavioral, and social-emotional interventions designed to address their unique needs.

Universal supports (Tier 1) are provided to all students during instruction of academic, behavioral, or social-emotional learning. Targeted supports (Tier 2) are used when the universal instructional supports and resources are not adequate to support a student's learning needs. Only some students should need these additional targeted supports and resources. Intensive supports and resources (Tier 3) are used when the targeted supports are not enough for the student to be successful. Students move up and down the continuum of universal, targeted, and intensive supports based on specific needs, not based on labels. A student who needs Tier 2 interventions in a certain mathematics concept receives that support on that topic only as long as needed and is not permanently labeled or given Tier 2 supports in every area.

Figure 4.1 (page 60) illustrates the correct vision of tiered supports and interventions from an MTSS perspective by showing how a single student receives supports in different tiers for different academic, behavioral, and social-emotional skills. For example, this student is receiving Tier 3 interventions for reading, Tier 2 supports for self-regulation and

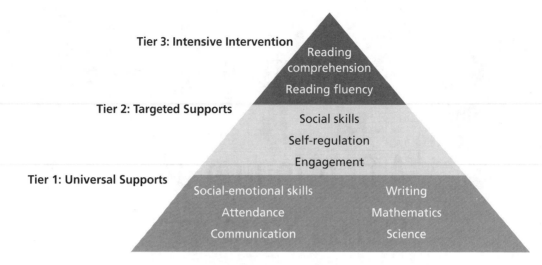

Figure 4.1: Variability of tiered supports for a given student.

engagement, but only requires Tier 1 (that is, universal) support for social-emotional skills, mathematics, and other areas. Tiers are designed to honor and support students' variability of strengths and challenges. Ultimately, supports are tiered, *not* students. This is a critically important point for a school or district; building an MTSS framework eliminates labels and serves students based on their learning needs.

Academic, Behavioral, and Social-Emotional Supports

Students vary in the degrees of academic, behavioral, and social-emotional support they need in any given instructional setting. Some students will not progress as expected, even though they receive high-quality universal instruction directed toward mastery of essential standards and skills for their grade level (Rogers et al., 2020). A three-tiered approach to supports and services helps educators identify and provide support at universal, targeted, and intensive levels. When students receive appropriate supports in a timely manner, fewer students need intensive or special education services (Maier et al., 2016). The three-tiered structure's most profound benefits are its preventative nature and rapid response to students' needs.

As mentioned in the introduction, a pyramid often represents the three-tiered approach. The division of the pyramid into Tier 1 (universal), Tier 2 (targeted), and Tier 3 (intensive) segments reflects the ideal percentage of students receiving services in each tier. For example, in a healthy model, at least 80 percent of students should be successful with only Tier 1 instruction and supports, as indicated by universal screeners. (If not, improving universal instruction and supports should be your highest priority, according to educator and author Terri Metcalf [2015a].) All students receive the benefits of effective and rigorous Tier 1 instruction, but we can expect that some students will still need additional support. To keep your MTSS model in balance, 15 percent or less of students should receive Tier 2 supports and 5 percent or less should receive Tier 3 interventions. Figure 4.2 details this concept.

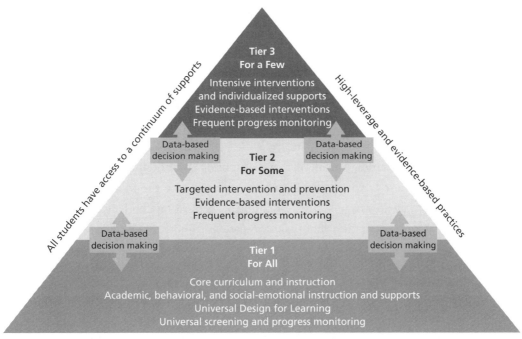

Figure 4.2: Continuum of tiered supports.

MTSS is a proactive and preventative model to ensure students do not fall so far behind that they cannot catch up and accelerate learning for those already behind (Maier et al., 2016). As described in the previous chapter (page 41), the core instruction in Tier 1 targets essential standards and is where prevention of learning loss through highly accessible teaching occurs. Per the principle of universal access, all students receive this instruction and all students are eligible for more intensive supports *if* their data show they need them. This concept is often misunderstood in the processes school systems use to identify students for special education. Many educators assume that students with special needs should be served at the Tier 3 level. We suggest that all students receive intervention and support services throughout the tiered continuum. Students with special needs, like all students, should receive all the benefits of Tier 1 instruction, supports, and resources, as well as Tier 2 and Tier 3 supports as needed. Tier 3 is not special education; Tier 3 is an intensive extension of the supports provided in lower tiers, focused on remediating learning skills. Another common misunderstanding is when schools provide Tier 2 or Tier 3 supports *in place of* Tier 1, removing students from core instruction time to receive intervention services.

Misconceptions of the tiered continuum of supports like these lead to unhealthy systems with a disproportionate number of students receiving Tier 2 and Tier 3 supports, as well as over-identification for special education. The three-tiered pyramid is only as strong as the foundation of Tier 1, where universally accessible instruction occurs. A framework without a strong foundation easily collapses under the pressure of having too many students at the higher levels. Due to the targeted and intensive nature of Tiers 2 and 3, providing these interventions for a large percentage of students is unstable and unsustainable.

With this overview in mind, read the following sections to learn more about the specifics of each tier.

Tier 1: Universal Access

As described in chapter 3 (page 41), Tier 1 is where universally accessible core instruction for *all* students occurs. Teachers use Tier 1 instructional time to prioritize essential standards and skills and design lessons with multiple means of instruction to support all students' learning opportunities. This is an area that most schools desire to achieve but struggle to implement (McCart & Miller, 2020). One must embrace the idea that *all* means *all*, inclusive of students who demonstrate academic and behavioral challenges. Tier 1 requires a unique approach to instruction that includes academic and behavioral learning. Students depend on it, and MTSS is built on it.

Teaching at Tier 1 refers to universal instruction, strategies, and interventions. RTI experts Austin Buffum, Mike Mattos, and Janet Malone (2018) suggest Tier 1 "teaching must include instruction on the skills, knowledge, and behaviors that a student must acquire during the current year to be prepared for the following year" (p. 20). These features distinguish Tier 1.

- Students receive multiple academic and behavioral or social-emotional supports.
- All staff deliver instruction using a high-quality framework, such as UDL.
- Grade-level or site screening teams screen all students and teachers monitor their students' progress on a regular and ongoing basis.
- Tier 1 remains accessible to all students even if they also receive Tier 2 or Tier 3 services.

Tier 2: Targeted Intervention

The targeted interventions of Tier 2 are for students who, based on universal screeners or key data indicators such as classroom formative assessments or skill-based assessments, have not responded to Tier 1 efforts. These students need a little more targeted help with content or skills that were recently taught or need targeted behavioral supports to help regulate their behavior. Tier 2 interventions are always provided in addition to universal supports, never in lieu of universal supports. Students should never miss universal instruction to receive Tier 2 services. Tier 2 provides a double dose of resources, supports, and interventions to meet students' needs. Usually, specially trained teachers and support staff provide research-based Tier 2 interventions. The classroom teacher must continue introducing new skills and content, but students receive Tier 2 interventions until they achieve mastery of the essential standards (Buffum et al., 2018).

For example, imagine a student who is referred to a Tier 2 mathematics intervention because he is struggling with basic operations and is therefore below grade level. In addition to the differentiated small-group instruction that occurs in class, the student receives additional interventions with a mathematics specialist three times per week for thirty minutes during the intervention time built into the master schedule. As another example, a student who consistently receives discipline referrals for her behavior on the playground might, in addition to the social skills curriculum and practices occurring in the classroom, work with the school counselor on social skills and playground rules two days per week for twenty minutes during recess until a reduction in referrals is evident.

Teams must determine the frequency and duration of Tier 2 interventions. *Frequency* is the number of days per week that the student receives the intervention. *Duration* is the length of time that the student receives the intervention or support. Research-based interventions usually include a recommended frequency and duration, but teams can determine within four to six weeks whether an intervention or support is working for the identified learning need. If students do not respond to Tier 2 interventions over a four- to six-week period or the predetermined amount of time defined for a certain research-based intervention, they may require Tier 3 support.

It's important to restate that *students* are not tiered. Supports provided within MTSS are based on each student's learning profile, which includes reporting on that student's academic, behavioral, and social-emotional past and current states, as well as any other contributing factors such as health, attendance, and any other information that will help put the appropriate supports in place for success. Students' learning profiles can be varied and contextually driven. Again, at any given time, a student may require different supports in different areas. For example, one student might receive Tier 2 academic supports to develop essential skills in the grade-level standards for mathematics and Tier 3 behavioral supports to address deregulated behaviors.

The following features distinguish Tier 2 targeted interventions.

- The intensity of services increases (for example, increased duration, increased frequency, targeted at specific skills).

- Progress-monitoring data are collected more frequently.

- Intervention is targeted explicitly toward academic or behavioral support.

- The most effective teachers and staff should provide targeted support.

- Students should work in smaller groups to address the area of need better.

- Intervention periods should be based on the frequency and duration of the intervention, resource, or support recommendations.

Tier 3: Intensive Intervention

Tier 3 interventions are for any students who require intensive remediation and did not respond to Tier 2 interventions (Maier et al., 2016). Deficits and struggles requiring Tier 3 support "are not skills and knowledge from the last lesson the teacher taught; they are from previous years—many times, from several years before" (Buffum et al., 2018, p. 28). Students needing intensive interventions often require more individualized supports; to accelerate their learning, teachers must discover what strategies and methods work best for them. Tier 3 services are a supplement to, not a replacement for, lower tiers. Students referred to Tier 3 intervention still receive Tier 1 instruction and Tier 2 supports. The intensive, evidence-based interventions of Tier 3 are also generally provided by specially trained teachers and support staff, such as literacy specialists or behavioral interventionists.

For example, imagine a middle school student who is far below grade level in literacy due to years of struggle with phonemic awareness. The student is still grappling with the sounds of the language instead of focusing on comprehending a text passage. This situation requires an intensive evidence-based intervention to accelerate the student's learning and build a strong foundation of literacy. While Tier 3 interventions are by definition time and labor intensive, recall that, in a healthy system, relatively few students should require Tier 3 interventions: "Providing all students access to essential grade-level curriculum and effective initial teaching during Tier 1 core instruction, as well as providing additional time and support to students at Tier 2, will result in success for most students" (Rogers et al., 2020, p. 7).

The following features distinguish Tier 3 interventions.

- Intervention is intensively focused by a teacher and provided to the student.
- Unique and specifically trained and skilled staff should provide Tier 3 supports.
- Group size should be small to allow for more intensive support.
- Intervention periods are longer in duration and more frequent in relation to Tier 2 intervention.
- Progress monitoring is conducted no less than once per week and may be more frequent.
- Students in Tier 3 should have a documented history of not responding to intervention at Tier 2.
- Interventions are selected based on student performance data showing why the student has not been successful.

Evidence-Based and High-Leverage Practices

In our descriptions of the three tiers, we did not identify any specific interventions or curricula as required for any of the tiers. This is because all instructional approaches and the continuum of supports should be responsive to students' current needs. Some school systems fall into the trap of designing their tiered continuum of supports based on certain programs. They build a pyramid of interventions and supports around programs the school has, instead of using the most appropriate evidenced-based interventions that strategically address student learning needs. For example, a school that has invested in a phonics program uses this program as its Tier 2 intervention for reading, even though student data indicate that some students have deficits in vocabulary, not phonics. This means that some students who need support do not respond to the intervention. A school with an effective MTSS framework would instead let student needs dictate what programs teachers use and would have multiple evidence-based interventions uniquely designed to address different student deficits. This holistic approach targets specific problems and builds tiers of intervention according to students' unique needs. Good interventions are responsive to students' academic, behavioral, and social-emotional needs based on data.

Good interventions are also backed by research showing their efficacy. We refer to these as *evidence-based practices*, and they are a critical component of an MTSS model. Specifically, evidence-based practices "have been shown in multiple rigorous research studies to improve student outcomes" (McIntosh & Goodman, 2016, p. 140). Unfortunately, many long-established practices that occur in schools and classrooms have no evidence of effectiveness (McIntosh & Goodman, 2016). It is critical as you embark on this work with your team that your team members become critical consumers of evidence-based practices. Being a critical consumer means understanding what evidence shows to be effective and implementable *with fidelity* (that is, implemented as prescribed to achieve the same effective results) within your school and district. By being informed, you won't be swayed into bringing costly, ineffective interventions into your district and schools by chance (Metcalf, 2015b).

Evidence-based practices are instructional practices that are content-specific and differentiated depending on the student's developmental level, which means that using the strategy must be appropriate to both the grade level and the skill. You wouldn't teach a high schooler a strategy for literacy that best supports students in fifth grade and below. There are also evidence-based practices that can most readily help targeted and intensive student needs. Specifically, evidence-based practices for at-risk groups, such as those students in special education, are instructional strategies backed by research and professional expertise to support the learning and behavior of students with disabilities (Cook, Tankersley, & Harjusola-Webb, 2008).

Another common term when it comes to interventions is *high-leverage practices*. The discussion around high-leverage practices has increased since the publication of *High-Leverage Practices in Special Education* (McLeskey et al., 2017) by the Council for Exceptional Children (CEC) and the CEEDAR Center. In this publication, the CEC and CEEDAR Center highlight four domains that research demonstrates can improve student achievement, regardless of content. In other words, these instructional practices result in higher student performance no matter the content area in which they are used. The report emphasizes high-leverage practices that are "intended to address the most critical practices that every K–12 special education teacher should master" (McLeskey et al., 2017, p. 11). We argue that the high-leverage practices identified for special education are also essential for general education and can help build a continuum of supports for all students. High-leverage practices provide the infrastructure support for effective teaching and learning for every child. The four domains indicated in the CEC and CEEDAR Center report are as follows (McLeskey et al., 2017).

1. **Collaboration:** How teachers collaborate with other professionals, families, and caregivers

2. **Assessment:** Formal and standardized assessments for informing ongoing supports and services

3. **Social-emotional and behavioral support:** How educators organize learning environments to promote student success

4. **Instruction:** The strategic application of content, pedagogy, lesson design, delivery, and evaluation

The book *Best Practices at Tier 3, Elementary* (Rogers et al., 2020) highlights research from the University of Michigan identifying the following nineteen high-leverage practices that are key to helping students learn academic and social-emotional competencies. (The order does not indicate significance; all high-leverage practices are equally important elements of effective teaching and learning; Rogers et al., 2020.)

1. Leading a group discussion

2. Explaining and modeling content, practices, and strategies

3. Implementing norms and routines for classroom discourse and work

4. Coordinating and adjusting instruction during a lesson

5. Specifying productive student behavior

6. Building respectful relationships with students

7. Talking about a student with parents or other caregivers

8. Learning about students' cultural, religious, family, intellectual, and personal experiences and resources for use during instruction (ensuring students are reflected in resources and materials)

9. Checking student understanding during and after lessons

10. Selecting and designing formal assessments of student learning

11. Interpreting the results of student work, including routine assignments, quizzes, tests, projects, and standardized assessments

12. Analyzing instruction to improve it

13. Eliciting and interpreting students' thinking

14. Diagnosing common patterns of student thinking and development in a subject matter domain

15. Providing oral and written feedback to students

16. Implementing organizational routines

17. Setting up and managing small-group work

18. Designing single lessons and sequences of lessons

19. Setting long- and short-term goals for students

This is not a definitive list of high-leverage practices. The CEEDAR Center (2017), for example, developed a crosswalk for high-leverage practices that helps to visualize the high-leverage practices in general education, the high-leverage practices in special education, and the related principal leadership practices for the success of students, especially those with disabilities. This document allows educational practitioners to select effective high-leverage practices that are consistent with research on learning and development and appropriate for students' needs. You can visit https://ceedar.education.ufl.edu/high-leverage-practices to access the crosswalk along with other resources on high-leverage practices.

Together, high-leverage practices and evidence-based practices can help form a continuum of tiered supports that build a robust MTSS framework. If MTSS is a framework that includes universal, targeted, and intensive supports, then evidence-based practices and high-leverage practices are the guidelines for how to design and implement the supports needed during instruction. As students move from Tier 1 (universal) to Tier 2 (targeted) and Tier 3 (intensive), they encounter more targeted and intensive evidence-based practices with greater frequency of high-leverage practices to enhance learning outcomes.

We recommend the following useful resources for selecting evidence-based practices for your continuum of supports.

- **What Works Clearinghouse (https://ies.ed.gov/ncee/wwc):** The What Works Clearinghouse's goal is to provide educators with the information they need to make evidence-based decisions. It uses high-quality research to determine what works in education. The website provides numerous evidence-based practices and intervention reports, practice guides, and individual study reviews.

- **IRIS Center (https://iris.peabody.vanderbilt.edu):** The IRIS Center provides educators with resources on effective evidence-based practices and interventions for improving outcomes for students, with an emphasis on students with disabilities.

- **National Center on Intensive Intervention (https://intensiveintervention .org):** The National Center on Intensive Intervention provides access to information on effective evidence-based intervention. It highlights various types of interventions most effective for improving student outcomes in English language arts, mathematics, behavior, and social-emotional learning.

As you begin your search, it is helpful to have a cursory overview of how evidence-based practices are rated. Typically, the type of evidence determines a practice's strength (and therefore its rating). Table 4.1 (page 68) describes how evidence-based practices are most often organized.

Table 4.1: Levels of Evidence

Level of Evidence	Type of Evidence	Strength of Evidence
Level 1	Well-designed, experimental, usually contains a randomized controlled trial	Usually considered *strong* evidence
Level 2	Will most often contain one quasi-experimental study	Usually considered *moderate* evidence
Level 3	Will most often contain at least one correlational study with controls for bias	Usually considered *promising* evidence
Level 4	Will likely need further investigations	Usually considered *relevant* evidence (demonstrates a rationale)

*Visit **go.SolutionTree.com/schoolimprovement** for a free reproducible version of this table.*

For educators, the main challenge is finding highly rated evidence-based practices for the type of learning deficits they are trying to address. There tends to be a more comprehensive array of level 1 and level 2 evidence-based practices available for elementary (K–5) contexts. Unfortunately, our experience with secondary (6–12) systems is that they have a much harder time finding practices that meet level 1 or level 2 evidence standards. As a result, they are more likely to resort to level 3 and level 4 evidence-based practices. However, the goal of building a continuum of tiered supports that addresses academic, behavioral, and social-emotional needs is not to find the perfect evidence-based practice, it's to help students. Some evidence is better than none. Educators must become knowledgeable about what to look for and how to analyze research to inform their choices regarding evidence-based practices. Over time, as teachers, leaders, and systems become more fluent in evidence-based and high-leverage practices, they can make better-informed decisions about which strategies and interventions to use. Figure 4.3 shows an example of assessing current high-leverage practices, and figure 4.4 (page 71) is a tool for assessing your evidence-based practices. Reproducible versions appear at the end of the chapter (page 80 and page 84).

High-leverage practices	Do you see this high-leverage practice used in your school? (Yes or no)	If yes, where do you specifically see that practice used consistently?	If no, why is the practice not being used?	What are the next steps to building consistent high-leverage practices?
Leading a group discussion	Yes	Some upper-grade classroom teachers use them.		Identify when all grade levels will use group discussion and for what purposes.
Explaining and modeling content, practices, and strategies	No		We do not have a consistent use of modeling.	Build modeling into lesson-plan development.

Eliciting and interpreting students' thinking	No		There is a lack of understanding among staff.	Provide professional training.
Diagnosing particular common patterns of student thinking and development in a subject matter domain	Yes	It happens often in science classrooms.		Have science teachers share with other teachers how they are using this high-leverage practice.
Implementing norms and routines for classroom discourse and work	Yes	All classrooms have norms and routines.		Discuss as a team what norms and routines we use.
Coordinating and adjusting instruction during a lesson	Yes	We are differentiating our lessons.		Explore if we are defining differentiation approaches the same way.
Specifying and reinforcing productive student behavior	No		We do not positively reinforce consistently as a staff.	Establish schoolwide behavior expectations.
Implementing organizational routines	Yes	All staff have been trained and are mentored in how to do this work.		n/a
Setting up and managing small group work	Yes	Some early grades are using small groups.		Not all small groups are effectively managed. Explore most consistent ways to manage small groups.
Building respectful relationships with students	Yes	All staff are focused on treating students and families with respect.		Survey students and families to see if they feel respected.
Talking about a student with parents or other caregivers	Yes	We have conferences with parents and caregivers regularly.		n/a
Learning about students' cultural, religious, family, intellectual, and personal experiences and resources for use in instruction	No		We don't have a way to do this consistently. We have cultural nights, but we aren't intentional about how to use those in our lessons.	Explore ways to embed students' cultures into lessons.

Figure 4.3: High-leverage practices inventory.

continued →

High-leverage practices	Do you see this high-leverage practice used in your school? (Yes or no)	If yes, where do you specifically see that practice used consistently?	If no, why is the practice not being used?	What are the next steps to building consistent high-leverage practices?
Setting long- and short-term learning goals for students	No		We are not consistent schoolwide in setting goals.	Establish clearly articulated goals and initiatives for our school.
Designing single lessons and sequences of lessons	Yes	All staff spend the beginning of each month's staff meeting reviewing lesson sequences.		n/a
Checking student understanding during and at the conclusion of lessons	No		This is not consistently done throughout every classroom.	Determine what effective checks for understanding look like.
Selecting and designing formal assessments of student learning	No		We are not designing common formative assessments.	Review common formative assessments and target expectations for use.
Interpreting the results of student work, including routine assignments, quizzes, tests, projects, and standardized assessments	Yes	All staff review student work and learn what needs to be done next for instruction.		Review how we are doing this together during collaboration time.
Providing oral and written feedback to students	No		We do not consistently provide oral feedback.	Review with leadership team what this means.
Analyzing instruction for the purpose of improving it	Yes	Upper-grade teams analyze instruction and make adjustments to instructional strategies.		Not consistently done; teams can review how we can be more systematic about this.

Source: Adapted from Rogers et al., 2020.

Evidence-based practice (title, description, document)	Evidence level (1–4)	Why is it used? What learning deficit are we targeting?	Who is responsible for monitoring fidelity of use?	Have we provided training, support, or oversight? If not, what do we need to do next?

Figure 4.4: Evidence-based practices inventory.

Resource Alignment

Whether you are redesigning your continuum of tiered supports or have just started thinking about tiered supports, it is a good idea to take a fresh and candid look at your current system. We know from our experiences initiating MTSS that it is vital to understand what instructional practices are currently in place and, notably, the people, time, and money available in each area to support student needs. How you choose to allocate your resources can profoundly impact whether or not your efforts will improve student outcomes. Whether you are well on your way to building an MTSS framework or just starting, it is helpful to understand your system's current reality. In the case of a continuum of tiered supports, it would help teams know what supports they have, why they have them, and where they fit in the continuum (at the universal, targeted, or intensive level). It is also helpful to understand what measurements or assessments you currently use to tell if students are improving and how your budget supports that alignment.

Going through this process raises several key considerations: What student data are guiding your initiatives and driving your funding allocations? What information is being used to determine the tiered intervention's effectiveness and supports? What time and people are being allocated to accomplish this work? How does your budget reflect your needs and priorities? Completing an inventory of your continuum of tiered supports answers these questions. A sample inventory appears in figure 4.5 (page 72), with a reproducible version at the end of the chapter (page 85). We encourage you to use the continuum of tiered supports inventory tool at both the district and school levels. This will allow your team to look at the entire school system to more readily identify gaps and opportunities to strengthen your continuum of tiered supports. As you complete the inventory, you will be able to see elements that are fully established and integrated within your system and areas that are missing or need to be revisited. This tool can help an MTSS improvement team more easily identify opportunities for improving the framework and student outcomes.

Tier 1	Academic Supports	Behavioral Supports	Social-Emotional Supports	Assessment Data	People, Time, and Funding Allocation
Universal Support Over 80 percent of students' needs are met in this universal support tier. This should include universal screening. This should also include a progress monitoring and benchmark tool at least three times a year.	Core Instruction Pedagogy and Curriculum: • UDL • KWL (Know, want to know, learned) chart • Explicit direct instruction	Core Instruction Pedagogy and Curriculum: • Classroom norms • Second Step behavior program	Core Instruction Pedagogy and Curriculum: • Class meeting check-in	• Common formative assessments • District benchmarks • State assessments	• $10,000 on substitutes, screening tool, data collection • $15,000 • Three days of professional learning on phonics skills
	Universal Screeners: • Dynamic Indicators of Basic Early Literacy Skills (DIBELS) • Accelerated Reader (AR) and STAR Reading tests	Universal Screeners: • Student risk screening scale	Universal Screeners: • Social skills improvement rating scales	• Screening data • Common formative assessments • Student goal setting	
	Interventions and Supports: • Scaffold vocabulary • Small-group standards reteach	Interventions and Supports: • Simple rewards incentive systems	Interventions and Supports: • Specific lessons from Second Step		• $12,000 for resources and trainers

Tier 2	Academic Supports	Behavioral Supports	Social-Emotional Supports	Assessment Data	People, Time, and Funding Allocation
Targeted Intervention Fifteen percent of students' needs are met in this targeted tier. Interventions should include supplemental progress monitoring at least once every four to six weeks. Tier 2 supports are provided in addition to Tier 1 supports.	Evidence-Based Practices: • Orton-Gillingham phonics instruction Progress Monitoring: • DIBELS • AR and STAR	Evidence-Based Practices: • Social-skills group Progress Monitoring: • Student-teacher tracker for desired behaviors	Evidence-Based Practices: • Class meeting check-in Progress Monitoring: • Social skills improvement rating scales assessment	• Common formative assessments • District benchmark assessments Progress-Monitoring Data: Intervention and curriculum-based progress-monitoring tools Curriculum-based measurement (CBM) Office discipline referrals Teacher surveys before and after behavior intervention period	• $10,000 for teachers to attend Orton-Gillingham training • $45,000 • Part-time intervention teacher • $20,000 for AR and STAR for every student • $5,000 for DIBELS materials and training
	Interventions and Supports: • Small group with similar skill needs	Interventions and Supports: • Check in–check out program • Nonverbal cues from teachers	Interventions and Supports: • Specific lessons from Second Step		

Figure 4.5: Continuum of tiered supports inventory.

continued →

Tier 3	Academic Supports	Behavioral Supports	Social-Emotional Supports	Assessment Data	People, Time, and Funding Allocation
Intensive Intervention Five percent of students' needs are met within this intensive tier. Individualize evidence-based practices to remediate and accelerate growth for academic and behavior support. Social-emotional interventions include individualized therapy or counseling, community services collaboration, and resources. Interventions should include supplemental progress monitoring weekly. Tier 3 supports are provided in addition to Tier 1 and Tier 2 supports.	Evidence-Based and High-Leverage Practices: • Direct instruction of skill • Increase in time and frequency of support • Instructional specialist or most skilled teacher in area provides intervention	Evidence-Based and High-Leverage Practices: • Targeted social skills lessons • Student behavior goal-setting charts supported with check in–check out	Evidence-Based and High Leverage Practices: • Targeted social skills lessons • Student behavior goal-setting charts supported with check in–check out	• Intervention assessment tool • Office discipline referrals	• $10,000 for teachers to attend intensive intervention training • $75,000 to hire a full-time school psychologist • Distribute counseling services to meet student needs at various schools • Professional learning days to train staff how to respond and support Tier 3 behaviors
	Progress Monitoring: • Frequent progress monitoring • Progress-monitoring tools provided with intervention curriculum • CBM	Progress Monitoring: • Frequent progress monitoring • Progress-monitoring tools provided with intervention curriculum • Office discipline referrals • Teacher and student data collection with check in–check out	Progress Monitoring: • Frequent progress monitoring • Progress-monitoring tools provided with intervention curriculum • Office discipline referrals • Teacher and student data collection with check in–check out	• Behavior reduction chart before, after, and during intervention	
	Interventions and Supports: • Small groups or one-on-one • Intervention is targeted to skill deficit • Frequency and duration of intervention is greater than Tier 2	Interventions and Supports: • Social skills small group • Behavior support plan • Supportive schedule with needed breaks or communication cards based on student need	Interventions and Supports: • Social skills small group • Behavior support plan • Supportive schedule with needed breaks or communication cards based on student need		

Tools for Building Your MTSS Framework

So far in this chapter we have discussed the essential components of a continuum of tiered supports and evidence-based practices. With this foundational knowledge, teams and schools can begin the journey of developing their own MTSS framework. To help you apply the element of a continuum of tiered supports in your organization, this section presents a case study, a team activity, a component audit, and an action plan.

Case Study

The following case study describes one approach to designing a continuum of tiered supports, integrating academic, behavioral, and social-emotional supports to form an improved MTSS framework.

Continuum of Tiered Supports

Robin Hood School is a K–5 school focused on building its student literacy. In the most recent statewide assessment, only 20 percent of students in grades 3–5 scored proficient in reading. The school team needed to do something drastic and realized they would have to be much more descriptive about how they organized their tiered support system for academic, behavioral, and social-emotional interventions. The team started by learning about what an effective MTSS program looks like. They quickly realized that their pyramid was upside down—most of their students were in a Tier 2 or Tier 3 intervention. Students were stagnant, not moving out of those tiers, and the bubble of students needing intensive supports was about to burst. School leadership quickly implemented an MTSS improvement team to assess the situation. The MTSS improvement team determined that the lack of support, resources, and effective Tier 1 (universal) instruction for reading created the demand for targeted and intensive supports. Knowing that this was unsustainable, the MTSS team quickly looked into high-leverage practices and evidence-based practices for improving literacy in upper-elementary students and found the following strategies.

- Use evidence-based and high-leverage practices.
  - ‣ Coordinate and adjust instruction during the lessons.
  - ‣ Set up small groups for literacy instruction.
  - ‣ Discuss with parents and caregivers students who were behind and needed extra support at home.
- Set long- and short-term reading goals with students and parents.
  - ‣ Use evidence-based practices.
  - ‣ Provide specific vocabulary instruction using a proven program.

‣ Teach students how to make inferences.

‣ Model good reading skills and acquire a supplemental research-based reading program.

‣ Teach students how to paraphrase using a proven strategy found on What Works Clearinghouse.

The MTSS improvement team began to build a more robust universal approach to literacy. The team consistently received feedback from the staff and parents; they also collected progress-monitoring data more frequently for Tier 2 and weekly for Tier 3. After six months, the team started to see some positive outcomes, and they began to feel more confident in their approach. However, they realized that students in Tier 3 often had other behaviors and social-emotional issues impeding their ability to learn. This prompted the team to look at some evidence-based, high-leverage practices for Tier 3 as well as evidence-based practices to address behavioral and social-emotional needs.

● High-leverage practices:

‣ Implement norms and routines for classroom discourse and work.

‣ Coordinate and adjust instruction during a lesson.

‣ Set short- and long-term goals for students and parents receiving Tier 3 behavior support.

‣ Learn about students' cultural, religious, family, intellectual, and personal experiences and resources for use in instruction.

● Evidence-based practices:

‣ Add a visual schedule to support students conceptualizing how the day will flow and help clarify expectations and provide opportunities for students to ask clarifying questions.

‣ Gather formative assessments with Tier 3 students, both with the whole class and in small groups, to adjust timing and pacing to support learning and positive behavior.

‣ Use a positive behavior goal-setting sheet so that the teacher, students, and families can monitor students' behavioral goals and progress in Tier 3 weekly.

‣ Utilize a student self-recording form, designed with an assets-based approach, to promote students' engagement, positive behavior, and school experiences.

At the end of the year, not everything was perfect. Robin Hood School's efforts were ongoing and still needed work. However, they accomplished a better, more coordinated continuum of supports using some high-leverage practices and evidence-based practices in daily instruction. For the MTSS improvement team, the efforts were considered a big win because, for the first time, they had a systematic approach for building a continuum of tiered supports.

This case study highlights the idea of not letting perfect be the enemy of progress. Robin Hood School, rather than focusing on getting everything right, chose to begin conversations and learning about evidence-based and high-leverage practices that could improve their continuum of tiered supports.

Answer the following questions about the case study and discuss them with your team. See page 88 for a reproducible version of these questions.

- What did you notice or learn from the case study?
- How does the case study exemplify the core components of this chapter?
- How do the team's actions in the case study serve the goal of ensuring all students learn?

Team Activity

The team activity allows you to reflect on what you have read and apply your team's learning. It is an opportunity to assess your organization's current state and decide the best next steps for building the continuum of tiered supports component of your MTSS framework. Each member should answer the questions in the team activity individually and then share responses with the team. See page 89 for a reproducible version of this activity.

- What portion of the chapter resonated with you most?
- What is your organization's current reality when it comes to a continuum of tiered supports?
- What do you think needs to change in your organization?
- What effective practices do you think need to continue in your organization?
- What steps do you suggest your organization take to improve the continuum of tiered supports?

Component Audit

The component audit for a continuum of tiered supports guides you to assess the most essential elements to build a strong foundation for the work ahead. After reading this chapter to learn about academic, behavioral, and social-emotional supports; evidence-based and high-leverage practices; and resource alignment, use the following steps to complete the component audit with your teams.

1. Have team members independently score the implementation status of each of the listed components in your school or district.

2. Compare scores within the team.

3. Discuss with your team to determine which component will be the most effective starting point—which one will have the biggest impact right now?

Figure 4.6 displays the component audit for a continuum of tiered supports. See page 90 for a reproducible version of this component audit.

Component	Essential Elements	Status
Academic, Behavioral, and Social-Emotional Supports Tiers of prevention and intervention to address learning gaps and behavioral challenges are in place.	• Teams or sites have a functional system that includes universal, targeted, and intensive levels. • There is structured time for students to participate in interventions without missing core instruction or cocurricular activities. • Stakeholders understand how decisions about which supports a student receives are made and adjusted.	☐ Not yet implemented ☐ Partially implemented ☐ Fully implemented ☐ Sustaining implementation
Evidence-Based and High-Leverage Practices Teams understand the importance of using practices that research has proven effective and have identified essential evidence-based and high-leverage practices for consistent use across the team or site.	• Teams utilize evidence-based practices and high-leverage practices in Tiers 1, 2, and 3. • Teams understand research-support ratings for evidence-based interventions.	☐ Not yet implemented ☐ Partially implemented ☐ Fully implemented ☐ Sustaining implementation
Resource Alignment The team has inventoried the school's tiered system of supports.	• Teams have inventoried the defined tiered supports: what they have, why they have it, and how it is used and funded. • Teams have connected the tiered inventory to student data, ensuring alignment between what is offered and what students need.	☐ Not yet implemented ☐ Partially implemented ☐ Fully implemented ☐ Sustaining Implementation

Figure 4.6: MTSS component audit—Continuum of tiered supports.

Action Plan

Based on the results of your team activity and component audit, develop your action plan for implementing a continuum of tiered supports, as shown in figure 4.7. A reproducible version appears on page 91. In this sample, the team identified evidence-based and high-leverage practices as their component that will have the biggest impact right now. The school has not used these practices before, so the team has identified two action steps to start building a base of knowledge.

Beginning date:	Continuum of Tiered Supports	Check when completed
_____	**Component:** Evidence-based and high-leverage practices (teams understand the importance of using practices that research has proven effective and have identified essential evidence-based and high-leverage practices for consistent use across the team or site)	
Action plan	Build understanding and practical knowledge of evidence-based and high-leverage practices in Tiers 1, 2, and 3. Collaborative teams will review and identify at least one evidence-based practice to implement during Tier 1 instruction, focusing on one each week as a team and discussing its use and effectiveness.	
	Build understanding of research-support ratings for evidence-based interventions. Each team will explore the National Center on Intensive Intervention (NCII) and provide a summary of the review of at least one evidence-based intervention.	
How will you monitor the implementation? What evidence will you examine?	• Through meeting notes, the team will document what they learned and will share with the improvement team what evidence-based interventions might be used to support their students in literacy and mathematics. • The improvement team will develop an action plan based on input from monthly staff meetings.	

Figure 4.7: Sample action plan for MTSS implementation—A continuum of tiered supports.

Summary

This chapter summarizes the essential elements of a continuum of tiered supports. We describe why three tiers of instructional interventions and evidence-based, high-leverage practices are essential to providing effective supports. All students receive high-quality instruction as part of Tier 1, and most students will be successful with these universal supports. Some students will need additional support and should receive targeted interventions in Tier 2. A few students will need intensive interventions to repair significant deficits, and these are the subject of Tier 3. The supports and interventions in every tier should be backed by research that confirms their efficacy.

High-Leverage Practices Inventory

As a team, review each of the high-leverage practices. Determine whether each practice is used consistently throughout the school. If yes, note which classrooms, teachers, teams, and so on use it consistently. If no, identify reasons why the practice is not consistent. In the last column, identify next steps that you could put in place to increase the consistency of the practice.

High-leverage practice	Do you see this high-leverage practice used in the school? (Yes or no)	If yes, where do you specifically see it being used consistently?	If no, why?	Next steps to build consistent high-leverage practices
Leading a group discussion				
Explaining and modeling content, practices, and strategies				
Eliciting and interpreting students' thinking				
Diagnosing particular common patterns of student thinking and development in a subject matter domain				

High-leverage practice	Do you see this high-leverage practice used in the school? (Yes or no)	If yes, where do you specifically see it being used consistently?	If no, why?	Next steps to build consistent high-leverage practices
Implementing norms and routines for classroom discourse and work				
Coordinating and adjusting instruction during a lesson				
Specifying and reinforcing productive student behavior				
Implementing organizational routines				
Setting up and managing small group work				

High-leverage practice	Do you see this high-leverage practice used in the school? (Yes or no)	If yes, where do you specifically see it being used consistently?	If no, why?	Next steps to build consistent high-leverage practices
Building respectful relationships with students				
Talking about a student with parents or other caregivers				
Learning about students' cultural, religious, family, intellectual, and personal experiences and resources for use in instruction				
Setting long- and short-term learning goals for students				
Designing single lessons and sequences of lessons				

Page 3 of 4

High-leverage practice	Do you see this high-leverage practice used in the school? (Yes or no)	If yes, where do you specifically see it being used consistently?	If no, why?	Next steps to build consistent high-leverage practices
Checking student understanding during and at the conclusion of lessons				
Selecting and designing formal assessments of student learning				
Interpreting the results of student work, including routine assignments, quizzes, tests, projects, and standardized assessments				
Providing oral and written feedback to students				
Analyzing instruction for the purpose of improving it				

Source: Adapted from Rogers, P., Smith, W. R., Buffum, A., & Mattos, M. (2020). Best practices at Tier 3: Intensive interventions for remediation, elementary. *Bloomington, IN: Solution Tree Press.*

Evidence-Based Practices Inventory

List the various evidence-based practices you are implementing in classrooms. Rate the quality of evidence (see table 4.1, page 68). Identify why each practice is being used and what specific skill it targets. List who is responsible for monitoring fidelity of use, then reflect on whether your team needs additional training, support, or oversight. Include any next steps.

Evidence-based practice (title, description, document)	Evidence quality rating (1–4)	Why is it used? What learning deficit are we targeting?	Who is responsible for monitoring fidelity of use?	Have we provided training, support, or oversight? If not, what do we need to do next?

Demystifying MTSS © 2023 Solution Tree Press • SolutionTree.com

Visit **go.SolutionTree.com/schoolimprovement** to download this free reproducible.

Continuum of Tiered Supports Inventory

Inventory the curriculum, resources, and support that your organization utilizes within each tier, including academic, behavior, and social-emotional elements. Identify all assessments being used in each tier and the data being collected. In the final column, list the people, time, and funding allocated to support each tier.

Tier 1

Tier 1	Academic Supports	Behavioral Supports	Social-Emotional Supports	Assessment Data	People, Time, and Funding Allocation
Universal Support Over 80 percent of students' needs are met in this universal support tier. This should include universal screening. This should also include a progress monitoring and benchmark tool at least three times a year.	Core Instruction Pedagogy and Curriculum:	Core Instruction Pedagogy and Curriculum:	Core Instruction Pedagogy and Curriculum:		
	Universal Screeners:	Universal Screeners:	Universal Screeners:		
	Interventions and Supports:	Interventions and Supports:	Interventions and Supports:		

Demystifying MTSS © 2023 Solution Tree Press • SolutionTree.com
Visit **go.SolutionTree.com/schoolimprovement** to download this free reproducible.

Tier 2

Tier 2	Academic Supports	Behavioral Supports	Social-Emotional Supports	Assessment Data	People, Time, and Funding Allocation
Targeted Intervention Fifteen percent of students' needs are met in this targeted tier. Interventions should include supplemental progress monitoring at least once every four to six weeks. Tier 2 supports are provided in addition to Tier 1 supports.	Evidence-Based Practices: Progress Monitoring: Interventions and Supports:	Evidence-Based Practices: Progress Monitoring: Interventions and Supports:	Evidence-Based Practices: Progress Monitoring: Interventions and Supports:		

Tier 3

Tier 3	Academic Supports	Behavioral Supports	Social-Emotional Supports	Assessment Data	People, Time, and Funding Allocation
Intensive Intervention Five percent of students' needs are met within this intensive tier. Individualize evidence-based practices to remediate and accelerate growth for academic and behavior support. Social-emotional interventions include individualized therapy or counseling, community services collaboration, and resources. Interventions should include supplemental progress monitoring weekly. Tier 3 supports are provided in addition to Tier 1 and Tier 2 supports.	Evidence-Based Practices: Progress Monitoring: Interventions and Supports:	Evidence-Based Practices: Progress Monitoring: Interventions and Supports:	Evidence-Based Practices: Progress Monitoring: Interventions and Supports:		

Chapter 4 Case Study Discussion Questions

Answer the following questions about the case study in chapter 4 (page 75) and discuss them with your team.

- What did you notice or learn from the case study?

- How does the case study exemplify the core components of this chapter?

- How do the team's actions in the case study serve the goal of ensuring all students learn?

Chapter 4 Team Activity: A Continuum of Tiered Supports

The team activity allows you to reflect on what you have read in chapter 4 and apply your team's learning. It is an opportunity to assess your organization's current state and decide the best next steps for building the continuum of tiered supports component of your MTSS framework. Each member should answer the questions in the team activity individually and then share responses with the team.

- What portion of the chapter resonated with you most?

- What is your organization's current reality when it comes to a continuum of tiered supports?

- What do you think needs to change in your organization?

- What effective practices do you think need to continue in your organization?

- What steps do you suggest your organization take to improve the continuum of tiered supports?

Chapter 4 Component Audit: A Continuum of Tiered Supports

To establish your current status with the continuum of tiered supports part of the MTSS framework, complete the following audit.

1. Have team members independently score the implementation status of each of the identified components in your school or district.

2. Compare scores within the team.

3. Discuss with your team to determine which component will be the most effective starting point—which one will have the biggest impact right now?

Component	Essential Elements	Status
Academic, Behavioral, and Social-Emotional Supports Tiers of prevention and intervention to address learning gaps and behavioral challenges are in place.	• Teams or sites have a functional system that includes universal, targeted, and intensive levels. • There is structured time for students to participate in interventions without missing core instruction or cocurricular activities. • Stakeholders understand how decisions about which supports a student receives are made and adjusted.	☐ Not yet implemented ☐ Partially implemented ☐ Fully implemented ☐ Sustaining implementation
Evidence-Based Practices Teams understand the importance of using practices that research has proven effective and have identified essential evidence-based and high-leverage practices for consistent use across the team or site.	• Teams utilize evidence-based practices and high-leverage practices in Tiers 1, 2, and 3. • Teams understand research-support ratings for evidence-based practices.	☐ Not yet implemented ☐ Partially implemented ☐ Fully implemented ☐ Sustaining implementation
Resource Alignment The team has inventoried the school's tiered system of supports.	• Teams have inventoried the defined tiered supports: what they have, why they have it, and how it is used and funded. • Teams have connected the tiered inventory to student data, ensuring alignment between what is offered and what students need.	☐ Not yet implemented ☐ Partially implemented ☐ Fully implemented ☐ Sustaining implementation

Chapter 4 Action Plan for MTSS Implementation:
A Continuum of Tiered Supports

Based on the results of your team activity and component audit, develop your action plan for implementing a continuum of tiered supports. Fill in the component of a continuum of tiered supports that you have selected as your focus. Then, list tangible actions that will help improve the status of this component in your school or district, perhaps using the essential elements listed in the component audit as a guide. Finally, define the evidence that you will use to monitor your progress. This action-plan template will build through each chapter into a strategic plan to set the course for long-term implementation.

Beginning date: _____	Continuum of Tiered Supports Component:	Check when completed
Action plan		
How will you monitor the implementation? What evidence will you examine?		

Data-Based Decision Making

Data-based decision making is one of the four essential components for building an effective MTSS framework. Austin Buffum, Mike Mattos, and Chris Weber (2009) define *data-based decision making* as "a continuous process of regularly collecting, summarizing, and analyzing information to guide development, implementation, and evaluation of an action; most importantly, this process is used to answer educational or socially important questions" (p. 206). In our MTSS framework, we expand the meaning of data-based decision making to include an intentional effort to build the capacity of collaborative teams and organizations to analyze, make meaning of, and apply data to improve instructional knowledge of students' learning needs. In addition, data-based decision making also requires a deep understanding of standards, curriculum, and high-quality assessments used to monitor student learning. You can think of data-based decision making as a large part of an educator's data literacy, assessing what students know and can do.

In this chapter, we review the importance of collaboration for data-based decision making and introduce the four steps to becoming a data-based decision-making team.

Collaboration and Data-Based Decision Making

Data-based decision making begins with the consistent habit of using data to drive instruction and initiatives to improve student achievement. Effective use of data will require educators to be intentional in analyzing and applying data to change their systems for improved student outcomes. This all sounds obvious when written on paper, yet the act of using data for sound data-based decision making is nothing of the sort.

The trend for data use in education has been to apply lessons from other institutions, such as healthcare fields' use of data, to what educators do (Bryk et al., 2015). This trend has generated buzzwords like *continuous improvement, continuous programmatic improvement, data literacy*, *data use*, and of course, *data-based decision making*. These multiple terms pulled from other disciplines can complicate the message, yet all of them are based on the premise of improved collaboration and outcomes based on data. As education professionals Ellen Beth Mandinach and Edith Gummer (2019) write, "The trend in education has become very clear of late. The push has been for education to become evidence-based, like other professions. This expectation has been the case for K–12 teachers, schools, and districts" (p. 3). Transferring best practices like data use from other fields is a daunting but a necessary task for implementing an effective MTSS framework. Teams and school systems will need to collaborate to be successful.

This section highlights the connection between data-based decision making and collaboration, such as the collaborative structures of a PLC process. Both high-quality instructional strategies and high-quality data processes depend on robust collaboration structures. Critical to MTSS is the connection teams make between data and instruction. The collaborative professional process asks its members to be transparent with student performance data and share ideas and best practices to improve the instructional practices of the entire team.

Data-based decision making is part of the systemic process of collaborative structures like PLCs. Collaborative teams basing decisions on data in service of learning is a foundational practice for MTSS. Data-based decision making focuses and inspires the collective action of collaborative teams, MTSS improvement teams, and all responsible for improving outcomes for students.

The best way to assess whether your collaborative teams are using a data-based decision-making process is to answer the following three questions.

1. Do instructional practices change as a result of the data the teams analyze?

2. Do team members collectively commit to data being part of every collaborative team?

3. Does the performance of students and the team improve as a result of the collaborative process and time working together?

The responses to these questions will guide next steps in determining what occurs when a collaborative team comes together. Effective teams will use student data to inform practice and instruction, making documentable, observable shifts in classroom practice in service of improving student outcomes.

While all components of the MTSS framework are essential, collaborative leadership structures and data-based decision making are especially intertwined. Each component depends on the other to strengthen educators' ability to improve student outcomes.

A Process for Data-Based Decision Making

Data-based decision making is an essential element in MTSS. When collaborative teams use data to understand student learning, guide daily instruction, and engage in continuous improvement, a data culture begins to form (Wayman, Midgley, & Stringfield, 2006).

Collaborative teams need to have reliable, consistent, and accessible data to ensure the choices and decisions teachers make can be analyzed over time to confirm actions are making a difference in student outcomes. Despite proliferation of available data and the importance placed on data-based decision making, there continue to be multiple barriers in school systems that prevent effective data-based decision making.

Researchers Raeal Moore and Michelle Croft (2018) identify major barriers for educators based on their roles: Teachers and principals report that the major barrier is the lack of time allocated to engage in data-based decision-making activities, while district administrators indicate both time and a lack of technical skills among school staff to access data or use electronic data platforms (Moore & Croft, 2018). Harvard Business Review Analytic Services (2019) discusses further barriers to data-based decision making in organizations and identifies the largest reported barrier associated with using data as a lack of organizational alignment and agility. So, how do we create better alignment and agility with data use? The following four-step process answers this question.

1. Understand quality assessments.

2. Use an assessment inventory to evaluate local assessments.

3. Build a data-discussion calendar to guide analysis of prioritized student data.

4. Apply a data protocol.

The following sections detail each step.

Understand Quality Assessments

The first step in data-based decision making is understanding what quality assessments are (McIntosh & Goodman, 2016). Quality assessments should meet the following criteria.

- **Valid:** The assessment measures what it is intended to measure.

- **Reliable:** The metrics are consistent each time the assessment is given.

- **Timely:** The assessment can be administered and the results interpreted in time to be useful.

- **Accessible:** The assessment and data are available to those who need the information to respond to student learning needs.

As teams begin to think about quality assessments, they sometimes realize that they use a high volume of assessments, but not high-quality ones. Such teams are "data rich but information poor" (DuFour et al., 2021, p. 21). In this instance, assessment data are plentiful yet not used to improve teacher instruction to impact student achievement.

For educator teams to anchor collaboration with data-based decision making, teams need access to high-quality assessments that generate data. High-quality assessments are always challenging as the term *high-quality* is usually up for interpretation. DuFour and colleagues (2021) call out the following principles to help educators enact high-quality assessments.

- It is best to assess only a few essential skills more frequently rather than many skills infrequently.

- Teachers need to have a clear idea of what students need to know and then develop or identify a good assessment to determine if students understand. Teachers need to be able to explain why and what students are learning in student-friendly ways.

- High-quality assessment provides a firm goal and flexible means for students to demonstrate learning. No single assessment is perfect, and therefore, multiple measures for student learning are needed.

- Most authentic assessments are open-ended and combine multiple ideas that students need to solve, therefore requiring students to apply their learning in a way that demonstrates substantive understanding.

- High-quality assessments are intentional in aligning classroom assessments and high-stakes tests.

- Assessments need to provide teachers information about student learning and students with input for reflecting on their learning progress.

- Assessments help differentiate between what students have learned in comparison to the intended learning or standard.

One common problem with assessment is a disconnect between district assessments and classroom assessments. When this occurs, it is often due to a lack of alignment between written curriculum, what is on the tests, and what is taught in the classroom. Another pitfall is when the assessment does not assess what it intends to. For example, an assessment asks students to write a paragraph about the characterization in a text, but the feedback addresses the structure of the writing or the grammar, rather than the standard on characterization.

In addition to understanding these characteristics of quality assessments, teams should be aware of different types of assessments, such as the following. Developing high-quality assessments requires knowing what types of assessments are available and how and when teams should use them.

- **Formative assessments:** Checkpoints to evaluate how students are learning the material throughout the unit or course (for example, exit tickets, whiteboard responses, and brief digital quizzes)

- **Summative assessments:** Measures of learning at the end of a unit or course (for example, end-of-unit assessments, comprehensive portfolios, and course final exams)

- **Qualitative data assessments:** Assessments that result in data other than a composite score or rubric score (for example, analysis of teaching artifacts, feedback forms, self-analysis, and survey data)

- **Quantitative data assessments:** Assessments that result in a composite score or rating (for example, rubrics, graded papers or tests, and online platform assessments)

All four of these assessment types can produce good and bad data, but understanding those data is essential to ensuring that teams have quality assessment data and use the suitable assessment to gather the correct information. For example, if a teacher wants to check whether students are progressing with the daily content, formative assessment would be the best approach.

Once teams understand what quality assessments are, they can evaluate their own use of assessments—what assessments they have, what they are assessing, the frequency or expectation of the assessments, and why they should be applied.

Use an Assessment Inventory to Evaluate Local Assessments

We recommend teams inventory their assessments at the classroom, school, district, and state levels to understand the purpose of those assessments and how they are used, as well as the frequency of administration. This process helps MTSS teams gain a clear picture of how many assessments students are taking and why they are taking them. Is it to guide teacher instruction? To determine what support students may need? For state or district accountability? What is the distribution of formative and summative assessments? What content is being assessed? Answering these questions can help identify redundancy, expose gaps in data, and highlight intense testing periods.

Completing the assessment inventory will provide your team and organization with a deeper understanding of assessment use across your system. In addition, it will help teams analyze the assessments for quality. The process of completing the inventory gives insights regarding the number, type, and purpose of assessments students are asked to complete. We recommend that teams engage in this process twice a year to build alignment. Figure 5.1 (page 98) displays a sample assessment inventory. A reproducible appears at the end of the chapter (page 109).

An assessment inventory can create coherence and help prevent becoming data rich but information poor. If a team understands which quality assessments it uses and for what purpose, the team can make better-informed decisions about the following questions.

- Do we need all these assessments?
- Can any assessments be combined?
- Do they assess what we think they assess?
- Can we access the results so we can use them?
- Are they valid, reliable, and timely?

Once teams inventory their assessments to understand their use and purpose, they are ready for a data-discussion calendar to further develop data-based decision making for MTSS improvement.

Assessment Inventory (PreK–3)

Grade	Academic Assessments	Behavioral Assessment	Social-Emotional Assessments	Frequency	Purpose
Preschool	• Desired Results Developmental Profile (DRDP) domains	• DRDP	• Desired Results Domains • Ages and Stages Questionnaire (ASQ)	• Fall (within sixty days of start of school) and spring (March or April) • Fall (within sixty days of start of school)	• Observe and assess students' skills and behaviors; DRDP informs instruction and state accountability. • DRDP informs teacher of social-emotional areas of strengths and challenges.
Transitional Kindergarten	• DRDP • Educational Software for Guiding Instruction (ESGI) • District benchmark assessments (DBAs)	• DRDP • Second Step	• DRDP • Second Step	• Fall (within sixty days of start of school) and spring (March or April)	• Observe and assess students' skills and behaviors; DRDP informs instruction and state accountability.
Kindergarten	• Teacher-made letters and letter sounds assessment (L/LS) • Basic Phonics Skills Test (BPST) • Dynamic Indicator of Basic Early Literacy Skills (DIBELS) • District benchmark assessments (DBAs)	• Schoolwide information system (SWIS) data analysis • Second Step	• Panorama SEL	• L/LS monthly until mastered • BPST monthly or as needed	• L/LS support teacher instruction and grade-level data to monitor student progress across classrooms. • BPST guides teacher instruction and districtwide analysis of foundational skills performance. • DIBELS guides teacher instruction and informs needs for continuum of supports for students and districtwide data analysis. • DBAs inform grade-level instructional planning and districtwide data analysis. • SWIS data address needed supports at the classroom, school, and district levels. • Second Step informs classroom-based instruction and needs for continuum of support students may need.

Grade	Assessments			Frequency	Use
First Grade	• Teacher-made letters and letter sounds assessment (L/LS) • Basic Phonics Skills Test (BPST) • Dynamic Indicator of Basic Early Literacy Skills (DIBELS) • District benchmark assessments (DBAs)	• Schoolwide information system (SWIS) data analysis • Second Step	• Panorama SEL	• L/LS monthly until mastered • BPST monthly or as needed • DIBELS three times per year • DBAs three times per year	• L/LS support teacher instruction and grade-level data to monitor student progress across classrooms. • BPST guides teacher instruction and report cards. • DBAs facilitate districtwide analysis of foundational skills performance. • DIBELS guides teacher instruction and informs needs for continuum of supports for students and district wide data analysis. • DBAs inform grade-level instructional planning and districtwide data analysis. • SWIS data address needed supports at the classroom, school, and district levels. • Second Step guides classroom-based instruction and informs needs for continuum of support students may need. • Panorama identifies behavioral and social-emotional support needs at the student, classroom, school, and district levels.
Second Grade	• Dynamic Indicator of Basic Early Literacy Skills (DIBELS) • District benchmark assessments (DBAs)	• Schoolwide information system (SWIS) data analysis • Second Step	• Panorama SEL	• DIBELS three times per year • DBA three times per year • SWIS weekly or biweekly • Second Step quarterly or as needed • Panorama three times per year	• DIBELS guides teacher instruction and informs needs for continuum of supports for students and districtwide data analysis. • DBAs inform grade-level instructional planning and districtwide data analysis. • SWIS data address needed supports at the classroom, school, and district levels. • Second Step guides classroom-based instruction and informs needs for continuum of support students may need. • Panorama identifies behavioral and social-emotional support needs at the student, classroom, school, and district levels.

Figure 5.1: Sample assessment inventory.

continued →

Grade	Academic Assessments	Behavioral Assessment	Social-Emotional Assessments	Frequency	Purpose
Third Grade	• Dynamic Indicator of Basic Early Literacy Skills (DIBELS) • District benchmark assessments (DBAs)	• Schoolwide information system (SWIS) data analysis • Seconc Step	• Panorama SEL	• DIBELS three times per year • DBA three times per year • SWIS weekly or biweekly • Second Step quarterly or as needed • Panorama three times per year	• DIBELS guides teacher instruction and informs needs for continuum of supports for students and districtwide data analysis. • DBAs inform grade-level instructional planning and districtwide data analysis. • SWIS data address needed supports at the classroom, school, and district levels. • Second Step guides classroom-based instruction and informs needs for continuum of support students may need. • Panorama identifies behavioral and social-emotional support needs at the student, classroom, school, and district levels.

Build a Data-Discussion Calendar

A data-discussion calendar is sometimes confused with an assessment calendar. An *assessment calendar* typically defines when assessments are administered. A *data-discussion calendar*, on the other hand, defines when a team will review, discuss, and analyze assessment results. Planning for data analysis in this way is an essential but often overlooked element of MTSS. A data-discussion calendar ensures that the team regularly returns to the data to evaluate student growth and continually cycles from analysis to action to reviewing results. The step of building a data-discussion calendar intentionally sets the stage for the continuous-improvement cycle.

A data-discussion calendar holds stakeholders accountable for administering, collecting, or reporting the assessment during the prescribed time frame. Often in our work with districts, we see teams collect data with no defined intention of ever systematically looking at the results. For example, a system that prioritizes balanced literacy as an initiative should have explicit resources, interventions, and supports. It should also have assessments that allow educators to analyze literacy data within a specified time frame so teams can determine the effectiveness of teaching and literacy strategies and make necessary adjustments. In many cases, what is missing is a system of accountability for collaborative teams so that educators intentionally analyze the specific student data collected. Figure 5.2 (page 102) shows how teams can organize a data-discussion calendar to systematically plan and prioritize their data review dates. (A blank reproducible version appears on page 110.) This data-discussion calendar reflects a commitment to review data across all teams within a school or district. In the example, January focuses on analyzing the universal screener results. This high school has decided that all collaborative teams will analyze the universal screener to assess students' progress in each subject area.

Building a data-discussion calendar can begin with state and federal accountability data. Consider the timing of when these data are collected and reported. Then, use your assessment inventory to schedule data analysis for school- and districtwide assessments. Be sure to stagger the data across the year as you add local measures and improvement data; avoid scheduling most assessments at the end of the year, for example.

Building a data-discussion calendar also allows teams to understand the volume of data collected. Often, we find that teams collect more data than they can analyze consistently. In most cases, teams only use high-stakes test results or benchmark accountability data as the primary way of determining their instructional effectiveness. This practice can lead to challenges when assessing the ongoing effectiveness of teaching and learning—more interim assessments provide more precise and timely data. However, teams should start with what they have and expand over time.

Month	Assessment Data to Review
January	Midyear universal screener data
February	Midyear district benchmark assessment data
	Formative assessment results for mathematics facts
	English learner state assessment data
March	Fourth-quarter attendance data
	Suspension and expulsion data
	Attendance data
April	RTI, PBIS, and SEL tier data
	Special education data
May	Parent survey data
June	State assessment data for English language arts and mathematics
July	State accountability data
	English learner reclassification data
August	Suspension and expulsion data for previous school year
September	Beginning-of-year universal screening data
October	RTI, PBIS, and SEL tier data
November	Beginning-of-year district benchmark assessment data
	Suspension and expulsion data
	Attendance data
	Special education data
December	On track for graduation numbers

Figure 5.2: Example of a school data-discussion calendar.

Apply a Data Protocol

The data-discussion calendar determines when teams will analyze data; a data protocol defines *how*. A data protocol guides teams to analyze and discuss the data. It provides some simple steps that distinguish observation, process, analysis, and decision making and move a team from admiring the data to acting on the data. Having a simple data protocol will help team members become more effective and efficient in continuous-improvement cycles (see chapter 6, page 117).

To prepare for data analysis, teams should clearly identify what information they are reviewing and any expectations or goals for the results. Teams might consider whether the data are for accountability or improvement, what goals they have related to the data, and whether a particular student population is in focus. The data protocol that we then recommend teams follow has three fundamental analysis questions, with second-level questions for specificity.

1. What are the data telling us?

   • Do we identify any trends, patterns, or themes?

   • Do the data create more questions?

2. What do we need to know?

- Is there a particular student group we need more information on?

- Is there any missing information that would help us be more effective?

- Can we visualize the data in order to be efficient?

3. What actions or next steps should we take?

- What should we do next?

- Who should do it?

- When should we do it?

- What can we learn, improve, or change?

One of the keys to continuous improvement is to keep it simple. There are many protocols available to educators, but in our experience, starting with a basic approach gives you and your team the most traction for improvement. You can always innovate later once the team has expanded its capacity.

Figure 5.3 (page 104) shows a sample data protocol tool. A reproducible version appears at the end of the chapter (page 111).

Moving quickly from analysis to action (and back again) helps teams build confidence in their collaborative data-based decision-making process. A data protocol—coupled with understanding quality assessments, utilizing an inventory of local assessments, and building a data-discussion calendar—can jump-start the process of building data-based decision-making practices. More importantly, a data protocol is an essential component of an MTSS framework.

Tools for Building Your MTSS Framework

So far in this chapter, we have discussed the essential component of data-based decision making and a process for systemic data analysis. With this foundational knowledge, teams and schools can begin the journey of developing their own MTSS framework. To help you apply the element of data-based decision making in your organization, this section presents a case study, a team activity, a component audit, and an action plan.

Case Study

The following case study describes one approach to implementing data-based decision making and the positive impact it had on a school.

Data Analyzed	What are the data telling us? Are there any considerations for certain student groups?	What did we find or discover? What do we still need to know?	What actions or next steps should we take?
DIBELS	**Kindergarten** • All students: 40 percent • Multilanguage learners: 6 percent • Students with disabilities: 2 percent • Socioeconomically disadvantaged: 25 percent **Grade 1** • All students: 56 percent • Multilanguage learners: 45 percent • Students with disabilities: 20 percent • Socioeconomically disadvantaged: 56 percent **Grade 2** • All students: 50 percent • Multilanguage learners: 45 percent • Students with disabilities: 10 percent • Socioeconomically disadvantaged: 25 percent **Grade 3** • All students: 60 percent • Multilanguage learners: 55 percent • Students with disabilities: 30 percent • Socioeconomically disadvantaged: 65 percent	• Did the proficient students participate in our preschool or transitional kindergarten program? • Do the students with individualized education plans (IEPs) have literacy foundation goals? • Has the number of students at benchmark generally increased every year? • Why do our multilanguage-learner students make gains then drop through the year?	• Revisit instructional strategies and curriculum being used to teach foundational literacy skills with literacy teachers and principals. • Determine whether designated language-development time is being allocated for multilanguage learners consistently. Have director check weekly instructional calendars.

Figure 5.3: Sample data protocol.

Data-Based Decision Making

Mr. Jones, principal of JJ High School (a large urban high school), knew he had a problem. The educator teams at JJ High did not use data to improve outcomes. During his first year as principal, Mr. Jones observed collaborative team meetings. He observed a few teams that brought classroom assessment results, but other than teachers looking at test scores and periodically asking how their peers achieved the results, their conversations lacked any substance that would help transform the school.

Mr. Jones knew in his second year that data would need to become a more significant focus of his high school if it were to improve. Mr. Jones assembled an MTSS improvement team and began the process of asking about the assessments they used. He started with simple questions: Do we know what assessments we use? Do we understand why we use them? Next, the team moved toward inventorying all the assessments with which they measured their school and student progress. JJ High School found they were data rich and information poor—they did not have systematic ways to process, analyze, and use data for improvement.

In response, Mr. Jones worked with his district office to prioritize building his collaborative team leaders' capability to understand what quality assessments look like and how to use them. Once the team leaders had a better understanding, they designed introductory trainings in their collaborative team meetings to help all teachers better understand why quality assessments are essential and what assessments each team member has and uses. This movement was not without resistance. Some team members felt they already did a great job using and analyzing their data. Some staff argued that their students scored higher than their peers, so there was no need for them to use data. However, nobody could deny that JJ High needed a more systematic approach.

At the end of the second year of Mr. Jones's tenure, his MTSS improvement team felt that the school had a much better handle on what assessments they used and what they would need to improve. In Mr. Jones's third year, his teams felt ready to build a data-discussion calendar and establish a data protocol. Mr. Jones and the MTSS improvement team determined what key data they would analyze and review throughout the year to inform the continuous improvement work at the school. They calendared existing, accessible data first, such as attendance, suspension, and students failing or at risk of failing (that is, the number of students receiving Ds and Fs) in English language arts and mathematics. JJ High's teams were asked to review these data collaboratively on specific calendar dates.

> Using the data protocol, teams processed data and provided the information from their meetings for the MTSS improvement team. The data protocol allowed JJ High to systematize how teams processed data, their suggestions, and their challenges. More importantly, the collaborative teams found challenges with how data were represented and provided feedback on how they wanted to visualize the data, what was confusing, and what the school could do as a system to better support the teams and their students.
>
> By the end of Mr. Jones's third year as principal, the teams at JJ High were more consistently analyzing, using, and acting on data. JJ High was becoming a data-literate school and was better equipped in its fourth year to refine the data inventory, calendar, and protocols the teams were using to become a more effective data-based decision-making team.

This case study highlights how a school leader and improvement team can focus on systematic changes to improve outcomes for students by conducting an audit of what assessments the school uses and looking at those results in a consistent manner. This approach will increase the school's ability to respond to student growth as well as provide supports for those students who are behind.

Answer the following questions about the case study and discuss them with your team. See page 112 for a reproducible version of these questions.

- What did you notice or learn from the case study?

- How does the case study exemplify the core components of this chapter?

- How do the team's actions in the case study serve the goal of ensuring all students learn?

Team Activity

The team activity allows you to reflect on what you have read and apply your team's learning. It is an opportunity to assess your organization's current state and decide the best next steps for building the data-based decision-making component of your MTSS framework. Each member should answer the questions in the team activity individually and then share responses with the team. See page 113 for a reproducible version of this activity.

- What portion of the chapter resonated with you most?

- What is your organization's current reality when it comes to data-based decision making?

- What do you think needs to change in your organization?

- What effective practices do you think need to continue in your organization?

- What steps do you suggest your organization take to improve data-based decision making?

Component Audit

The component audit for data-based decision making guides you to assess the most essential elements to build a strong foundation for the work ahead. After reading this chapter to learn about understanding quality assessment, using an assessment inventory, building a data-discussion calendar, and applying a data protocol, use the following steps to complete the component audit with your teams.

1. Have team members independently score the implementation status of each of the listed components in your school or district.

2. Compare scores within the team.

3. Discuss with your team to determine which component will be the most effective starting point—which one will have the biggest impact right now?

Figure 5.4 displays the component audit for data-based decision making. See page 114 for a reproducible version of this component audit.

Action Plan

Based on the results of your team activity and component audit, develop your action plan for implementing data-based decision making, as exemplified in figure 5.5 (page 108). A reproducible version appears on page 115. In this sample, the team has decided to focus on applying a data protocol. Based on that component, they have defined several action steps and a monitoring plan that will help them improve their implementation status.

Component	Essential Elements	Status
Understanding Quality Assessments Collaborative teams understand what quality assessments are and how to use them.	• Teacher teams understand and use a variety of assessments, such as summative, formative, qualitative, and quantitative. • Teachers assess students frequently to acquire timely data.	☐ Not yet implemented ☐ Partially implemented ☐ Fully implemented ☐ Sustaining implementation
Using an Assessment Inventory Teams create a list of all classroom, school, district, and state assessments students take, what the purpose of each assessment is, who uses the data, and for what purpose.	• Teacher teams use assessment inventories to determine what assessments they have and their purpose. • Schools or districts ensure that students are not over-assessed and that assessments are meaningful to learning and instruction.	☐ Not yet implemented ☐ Partially implemented ☐ Fully implemented ☐ Sustaining implementation

Figure 5.4: MTSS component audit—Data-based decision making.

continued →

Building a Data-Discussion Calendar The staff understand what assessment data teams and the school will review for accountability and improvement and when.	• Teams have a data-discussion calendar showing the essential data that need to be analyzed. • Teams have a clear understanding of which data are for accountability and which data are for improvement.	☐ Not yet implemented ☐ Partially implemented ☐ Fully implemented ☐ Sustaining implementation
Applying a Data Protocol Teams use a consistent protocol for processing data through discussions.	• Teams have a process for analyzing and discussing student data. • Schools or districts have a standard data protocol that is used as a feedback loop with teams.	☐ Not yet implemented ☐ Partially implemented ☐ Fully implemented ☐ Sustaining implementation

Beginning date: _____	Data-based decision making **Component:** Applying a data protocol (teams use a consistent protocol for processing data through discussions)	Check when completed
Action plan	Ensure teams have a process for analyzing and discussing student data. Collect artifacts from data processes that teams are currently using and apply them as a basis for standardizing the protocol.	
	Schools or districts implement a standard data protocol that they use as a feedback loop with teams. The principal will look into professional learning about quality assessments and student data analysis.	
How will you monitor the implementation? What evidence will you examine?	• Develop a data protocol for the MTSS improvement team to test. • Examine artifacts such as templates, notes, and outcomes.	

Figure 5.5: Sample action plan for MTSS implementation—Data-based decision making.

Summary

This chapter discusses the essential component of data-based decision making. For schools and districts to make improvements in student outcomes, educators will need to be well versed in the assessments they are giving, why they are giving them, and how are they using the data to improve instruction and learning. This process entails a consistent cadence of regularly scheduled data reviews and a protocol to analyze data, enabling educators to gain a clear understanding of how students are progressing in their learning as well as early alerts to prevent student failure.

Assessment Inventory

For each grade level, identify all academic, behavioral, and social-emotional assessments that students take. For each assessment, define the frequency with which that assessment is given and the purpose for it.

Grade	Academic Assessments	Behavioral Assessments	Social-Emotional Assessments	Frequency	Purpose

Data-Discussion Calendar

Use the completed assessment inventory, as well as any other key decision-making data, to fill in the calendar of when that data will be reviewed and analyzed. Teams may decide to build a data-discussion calendar by grade level, school, and district. Different grade levels, departments, and schools can coordinate to review intersecting data in the same month.

Month	Assessment Data to Review
January	
February	
March	
April	
May	
June	
July	
August	
September	
October	
November	
December	

Demystifying MTSS © 2023 Solution Tree Press • SolutionTree.com

Visit **go.SolutionTree.com/schoolimprovement** to download this free reproducible.

Data Protocol

In the first column, identify what data you are analyzing. Include a narrative of the expected results. Transfer key data, patterns, trends, and outliers of student performance into the second column. Disaggregate the data in order to analyze the performance of different student groups. In the third column, summarize findings and discoveries from the analysis, as well as any information you still need to know or that the current data do not answer. Then, identify next steps as a result of the complete analysis and reflection.

Data Analyzed Expected Outcomes	What are the data telling us? Are there any considerations for certain student groups?	What did we find or discover? What do we still need to know?	What actions or next steps should we take?

Chapter 5 Case Study Discussion Questions

Answer the following questions about the case study in chapter 5 (page 103) and discuss them with your team.

- What did you notice or learn from the case study?

- How does the case study exemplify the core components of this chapter?

- How do the team's actions in the case study serve the goal of ensuring all students learn?

Chapter 5 Team Activity: Data-Based Decision Making

The team activity allows you to reflect on what you have read in chapter 5 and apply your team's learning. It is an opportunity to assess your organization's current state and decide the best next steps for building the data-based decision-making component of your MTSS framework. Each member should answer the questions in the team activity individually and then share responses with the team.

- What portion of the chapter resonated with you most?

- What is your organization's current reality when it comes to data-based decision making?

- What do you think needs to change in your organization?

- What effective practices do you think need to continue in your organization?

- What steps do you suggest your organization take to improve data-based decision making?

Chapter 5 Component Audit:
Data-Based Decision Making

To establish your current status with the data-based decision-making part of the MTSS framework, complete the following audit.

1. Have team members independently score the implementation status of each of the identified components in your school or district.

2. Compare scores within the team.

3. Discuss with your team to determine which component will be the most effective starting point—which one will have the biggest impact right now?

Component	Essential Elements	Status
Understanding Quality Assessments Collaborative teams understand what quality assessments are and how to use them.	• Teacher teams understand and use a variety of assessments, such as summative, formative, qualitative, and quantitative. • Teachers assess students frequently to acquire timely data.	☐ Not yet implemented ☐ Partially implemented ☐ Fully implemented ☐ Sustaining implementation
Using an Assessment Inventory Teams create a list of all classroom, school, district, and state assessments students take, what the purpose of each assessment is, who uses the data, and for what purpose.	• Teacher teams use assessment inventories to determine what assessments they have and their purpose. • Schools or districts ensure that students are not over-assessed and that assessments are meaningful to learning and instruction.	☐ Not yet implemented ☐ Partially implemented ☐ Fully implemented ☐ Sustaining implementation
Building a Data-Discussion Calendar The staff understand what assessment data teams and the school will review for accountability and improvement and when.	• Teams have a data-discussion calendar showing the essential data that need to be analyzed. • Teams have a clear understanding of which data are for accountability and which data are for improvement.	☐ Not yet implemented ☐ Partially implemented ☐ Fully implemented ☐ Sustaining implementation
Applying a Data Protocol Teams use a consistent protocol for processing data through discussions.	• Teams have a process for analyzing and discussing student data. • Schools or districts have a standard data protocol that they use as a feedback loop with teams.	☐ Not yet implemented ☐ Partially implemented ☐ Fully implemented ☐ Sustaining implementation

Chapter 5 Action Plan for MTSS Implementation: Data-Based Decision Making

Based on the results of your team activity and component audit, develop your action plan for implementing data-based decision making. Fill in the component of data-based decision making that you have selected as your focus. Then, list tangible actions that will help improve the status of this component in your school or district, perhaps using the essential elements listed in the component audit as a guide. Finally, define the evidence that you will use to monitor your progress. This action-plan template will build through each chapter into a strategic plan to set the course for long-term implementation.

Beginning date: _____	Data-based Decision Making Component:	Check when completed
Action plan		
How will you monitor the implementation? What evidence will you examine?		

Chapter 6

Continuous Improvement for Sustaining MTSS

The previous four chapters described the four essential elements of our MTSS framework: collaborative leadership, universal access, a continuum of tiered supports, and data-based decision making. Continuous improvement is the process that brings them all together and sustains the system. We devote this chapter to continuous improvement to highlight its important components, though it applies to and is embedded in all parts of the framework. Whether you are implementing collaborative leadership, building universal access, defining a continuum of supports, or engaging in data-based decision making, each of these should include a form of evaluation using continuous improvement. The term *continuous improvement* is used in education to describe a multitude of actions and behaviors related to schools and districts becoming learning organizations that use self-reflection and systems analysis to improve outcomes for students (Bryk et al., 2015; Langley et al., 2009). Models such as Plan-Do-Study-Act and design, deliver, debrief are common implementations of this concept (Bryk et al., 2015). *Continuous improvement* is a very broad term to describe what should be a complex cycle of inquiry. In *Learning to Improve*, Bryk and colleagues (2015) describe continuous improvement as using research knowledge that produces multiple cycles of inquiry over a period of time.

For educators to build an MTSS framework that uses continuous improvement, teams must understand its application in daily classroom and organizational practices. In this chapter, we explore what continuous improvement is and what it looks like in practice, specifically within collaborative leadership structures, and how each team (including MTSS improvement teams, teacher teams, site leadership teams, and district leadership teams) contributes to the systemwide accountability and sustainability of MTSS. We share processes for continuous improvement that enable you to evaluate current organizational structures, identify gaps, and design plans to improve the components of your MTSS framework.

Continuous Improvement Defined

The concept of continuous improvement originated with public health organizations and hospitals looking for a system or process to reduce the number of medical errors occurring while increasing the efficiency and effectiveness of the patient experience. As a result of the successes of continuous improvement in the medical field, education looked toward this model and how it could improve educational systems to increase student achievement outcomes (Bryk et al., 2015). The basic tenets of continuous improvement include addressing the root cause of a problem, applying a theory of improvement and change, and implementing that change in rapid cycles of improvement and evaluation. Bryk and colleagues (2015) call this shift in how educators address improvement "learning fast to implement well" (p. 7). The authors also want educators to recognize in their pursuit of improvement that "the system . . . produces the current outcomes" (p. 57). Bryk and colleagues (2015) highlight that in a culture of continuous improvement, educators realize there is no time to waste in pursuit of student improvement and the organization should no longer be allowed to default to "this is how we've always done it" practices, especially when those practices fail students.

There are many models of continuous improvement used in various fields. The following are a few examples of different improvement models.

- Network improvement communities (NICs) help build a focused team around a particular problem. NICs leverage the network of several collaborative teams focused on one aim to accelerate the learning by learning with and from each other (Bryk et al., 2015).

- Design-based implementation research helps build knowledge around specific problems of practice (Mandinach & Gummer, 2019).

- Deliverology focuses on system-level goals and planning and how to best deliver on those efforts (Barber, Rodriguez, & Artis, 2016).

- Implementation science focuses on fidelity of implementation of specific programs, interventions, or practices (Bryk et al., 2015).

- Lean improvement focuses on engaging participants in focused analysis of a specific problem through evaluation and reiteration to reduce complexities and unnecessary efforts (Mandinach & Gummer, 2019).

- Lean Six Sigma works to enhance the organizational process by reducing redundancy (Mandinach & Gummer, 2019).

Despite these many different forms, the key is fully understanding how to make continuous improvement work systematically in an MTSS framework.

In order to fully understand continuous improvement, it is important to quickly revisit what an MTSS framework is supposed to do. A comprehensive MTSS framework addresses students' needs no matter what degree of acceleration or remediation they need. MTSS should offer a tiered support system so that students receive academic and behavioral support at the level of intensity and frequency that is necessary for them to be successful. The foundation of MTSS is a strong, prevention-focused core instructional program at Tier 1. The structures and processes of continuous improvement are designed to support organizations in becoming *learning organizations*, consistently able to refine and adjust practices. In an MTSS framework, educators use data continually to adjust and refine systems in service of improving outcomes for all students.

Simply stated, continuous improvement is *getting better at getting better* (Bryk et al., 2015). So how do you begin the process of getting better at getting better? It starts with analyzing data. If collaborative teams are not using student learning data to guide their conversations (as described in chapter 5, page 93), it is impossible to form a strong MTSS framework or use a continuous-improvement process. Organizations that successfully sustain student improvement and meaningful tiers of support use data to drive learning from successes and failures. This allows the team to establish new iterations, practices, and designs for improvement: "Fundamental to data use is the concept of an integrative cycle of inquiry or a process of feedback that leads to continuous improvement" (Mandinach & Gummer, 2019, p. 8). The data-informed model of continuous improvement we espouse here builds on Peter Senge's 1990 work on organizational change (as cited in Mandinach & Gummer, 2019), which prioritizes feedback loops and data as mechanisms for improvement. This approach requires a shift from traditional educational operating procedures.

Traditionally, practitioners in education have been guided by superficial adjustments in policies and practices rather than engaging in deep systemic change. Government regulations have made attempts in mandating change with little success. School leaders have sought inspirational speakers, staff buy-in, and compliance to create change with limited positive outcomes or sustainability (Adelman & Taylor, 2018; Reeves, 2021). In our work, we have often observed traditional educational systems piloting initiatives when they want to try new investments, design new programs, and build new structures for learning. A *pilot* is when a small number of educators volunteer to engage in a cycle of inquiry in order to inform the larger school system about the effectiveness of an instructional practice. Piloting ideas and programs can be very useful in education for establishing the long-term impact of new ideas. However, in our experience, piloting does not work well for rapid cycles of inquiry. Often, traditional pilot programs wait too long to evaluate the effectiveness, and in many cases the commitment to the program has already been made. The investment of time and energy leaves little room to re-evaluate, change direction, or even accept that the program may not work. In contrast, continuous improvement recommends small cycles of inquiry to determine if the program is worth spreading and scaling the efforts.

To enact continuous improvement in your MTSS framework, we recommend using multiple smaller test cycles that focus on specific data you want to improve. Using the short, frequent cycles of the Plan-Do-Study-Act model enables individuals and teams to gain information quickly and produce scalable approaches and opportunities (Bryk et al., 2015). In other words, many small learning cycles working together can produce large system improvements while preventing the waste of time and resources on actions that may not work. Figure 6.1 depicts how small PDSA cycles generate larger changes.

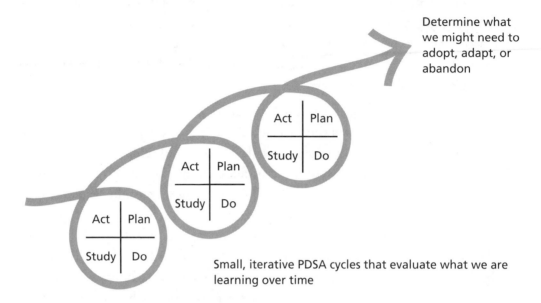

Source: Adapted from Institute for Healthcare Improvement, n.d.

Figure 6.1: PDSA cycles for continuous improvement.

This figure depicts small PDSA cycles that work together toward an incremental improvement effort. Similarly, collaborative team structures enable smaller groups to make a collective impact on the larger system. Thus, by conducting PDSA cycles within collaborative teams, educators can learn and generate input to improve the organizational MTSS framework based on practices that work.

The Plan-Do-Study-Act Cycle for Collaborative Teams

The use of continuous-improvement methodologies integrates with collaborative leadership structures. In organizations that embody the practice of continuous improvement, collaborative teams must use student learning data to continually inform and adjust their instructional practices, thereby analyzing the impact of those instructional adjustments. If the adjustments result in increased student achievement, teams either adopt that practice or innovate further to see if they can increase student learning even more. When new practices fail to improve student outcomes, teams abandon them, which is key to preventing ineffective instructional practices from becoming embedded within the team. The steps of the PDSA cycle are as follows (Bryk et al., 2015; Hall, 2016).

- **Plan:** Identify the problem or goal and determine what strategy to trial, who will conduct the trial, the time frame for the cycle, and any other relevant details.

- **Do:** Conduct the trial as designed in the Plan step. Be sure to collect preassessment and postassessment data.

- **Study:** Review the student data and discuss the results. Did the trialed strategy produce a positive, negative, neutral, or unknown effect?

- **Act:** Make a decision based on the outcome of the Study step. The team may decide to adopt, adapt, or abandon the trialed strategy, or to investigate it further.

For example, a school may want to test a new instructional strategy to determine if student engagement increases. Rather than select an instructional strategy that the whole school would use immediately, the school teams determine that a few teachers will test the strategy over a given week, collecting student responses of how they enjoyed the activity and analyze student results. The teachers share those results at the next collaborative team meeting and the team finds that the responses are positive. Therefore, more teachers within the team try the strategy. In this example, the idea is quickly tested, analyzed, and evaluated for expansion or elimination.

In the PLC process, our recommended model of collaboration, the continuous-improvement approach of analyzing student data, adapting instructional practices, and abandoning ineffective practices aligns directly with the four critical questions of a PLC (DuFour et al., 2016). Table 6.1 depicts this alignment.

Table 6.1: Continuous Improvement and the Critical Questions of a PLC

PDSA Step	PLC Questions	Team Actions
Plan	What is it we want our students to know and be able to do?	Identify standards and how students will demonstrate mastery of standards.
Do	What is it we want our students to know and be able to do?	Deliver instructional strategies, practices, and agreements.
Study	How will we know if each student has learned it?	Analyze assessment results.
Act	How will we respond when some students do not learn it? How will we extend the learning for students who have demonstrated proficiency?	Adopt, adapt, or abandon new strategies.

*Visit **go.SolutionTree.com** for a free reproducible version of this table.*

Collaborative teams that engage in PDSA improvement cycles aligned with the four critical questions demonstrate the process of continuous improvement. In the next section, we explore how PDSA cycles build on each other to generate larger improvements for your MTSS framework.

Effective Feedback Loops

To sustain an MTSS framework, leaders must purposefully engage teams in periodic, schoolwide cycles of continuous improvement. As Buffum and colleagues (2018) note, "The key to team success lies in the development of *systematic processes*—foundational structures that promote consistency, honest communication, respect, and mutual accountability within each team" (p. 61). To coordinate teams' PDSA cycles for larger improvements, our framework employs a systematic process called *collaborative team feedback loops*. Feedback loops are a system-level approach to prioritizing what a school or district wants to improve. They relate closely to the work of MTSS improvement teams and how they coordinate focus, clarify initiatives, and engage collaborative teams. For example, in a feedback loop a collaborative team uses data to analyze practices, test new strategies and practices to improve student outcomes, and share its findings with the schoolwide MTSS improvement team. The MTSS improvement team then analyzes and reviews this feedback collectively with other collaborative team feedback. Leadership then shares the ideas and discoveries throughout the school and guides decisions as to which ideas are worth schoolwide investments of time, resources, and funding. This feedback loop is dependent on grade-level or content-area collaborative teams providing information to MTSS improvement teams. MTSS improvement teams and leadership teams then need to evaluate the learning of collaborative teams and provide feedback to the whole site.

The MTSS improvement team can use the following three questions, adapted for schools and districts from the Institute for Healthcare Improvement (2003), to guide the development of feedback loops.

1. What are we trying to accomplish or improve as a school or district?

2. How will we measure our improvement as a school or district?

3. What changes can we make as a school or district that will result in the improvement we want?

These questions focus the improvement team's efforts and allow it to provide more specific guidance to collaborative teams. Once an MTSS improvement team identifies what it wants to accomplish or improve, it can then identify the data that best measure the system's collective improvement efforts, perhaps using the data-discussion calendar (chapter 5, page 93) to review which data are consistently available. Individual collaborative teams can then use the data protocol (page 102) to review their data and engage in periodic schoolwide discussion of the organizational priorities. Collaborative teams can give input and then test ideas in a PDSA cycle for systemwide changes that lead to adopt-or-abandon decisions. Figure 6.2 displays the collaborative team feedback loop that enables systemwide continuous improvement.

For example, if a district was trying to reduce chronic absenteeism systemwide, the schools within the district could ask their collaborative teams to review data on attendance rates. Specifically, teams could look at school-level data and collaborative team data, using the

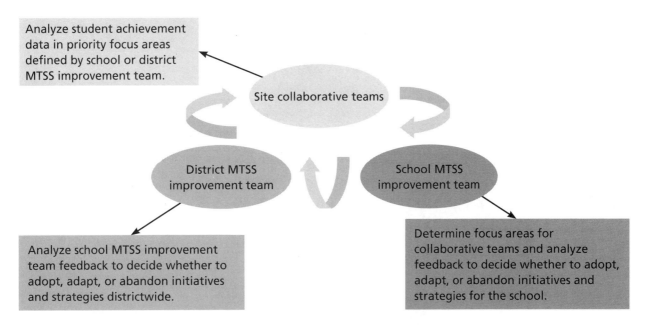

Figure 6.2: Collaborative team feedback loop.

data protocol to guide their conversations. Teacher teams would then offer feedback to the school's MTSS improvement team, which would aggregate that feedback and share it with the district. Thus, collaborative team inputs help guide larger system improvement efforts. The district team might identify an evidence-based practice designed to address chronic attendance issues and share it with school-level MTSS improvement teams. The school team disseminates the initiative to teacher teams, which use PDSA cycles to test the strategy. Then, the school team collects and analyzes the data from the collaborative teams and shares that data analysis with teachers and district. Ultimately, the schools and district determine whether the strategy should be adopted, adapted, or abandoned. Such a feedback loop could be repeated throughout the year with further changes designed to address chronic attendance issues. Together, the entire system can better support teachers, students, and families in improving student attendance.

The feedback loop process allows schools within a district to be part of a coherent and systemic effort to improve a challenge the district is experiencing. The information that flows through the feedback loop—consisting of ideas for student improvement and data that result from testing them—allows whole systems to generate improvement in their MTSS frameworks.

Tools for Building Your MTSS Framework

So far in this chapter, we have discussed continuous improvement, PDSA cycles, and feedback loops. With this foundational knowledge, teams and schools can begin the journey of sustaining their own MTSS framework. To help you apply the concept of continuous improvement in your organization, this section presents a case study, a team activity, a component audit, and an action plan.

Case Study

The following case study exemplifies continuous improvement within an MTSS framework.

Continuous Improvement

Xander Unified School District sought to build an MTSS framework. In doing so, leaders realized there were several foundational elements they needed to enhance so they could support schools in building an MTSS framework. The district invested time and energy into building collaborative structures, data-based decision making, and tiered supports. While it was building these essential components, the district wanted to integrate continuous-improvement feedback loops that connect PDSA cycles from the classroom to the school to the district office.

First, the district formed an MTSS improvement team and selected a focus area for improvement. The district team decided to focus on suspension and expulsion rates, with an emphasis on students with disabilities. Second, the district added the focus area to the shared district data-discussion calendar so site leaders and collaborative teams would know when the district would be reviewing data on suspension and expulsion. Third, the district worked with site leaders to identify when teacher and school teams would review their respective grade-level and site data, as this would need to occur before each district MTSS team review. Fourth, the district team provided a data protocol for collaborative teams to use when discussing suspension and expulsion data. Fifth, to gather feedback from school sites, the district MTSS team asked school MTSS improvement teams to consolidate the information from collaborative team discussions.

Once they collected this feedback, the district MTSS improvement team met to synthesize the data from the different schools. The team then shared this information with the site leaders and collaborative teams in order to form a feedback loop with site and collaborative teams. The district MTSS improvement team used three questions to guide their feedback and build awareness based on the feedback cycles from the schools.

1. What should the district MTSS team test or adopt?

2. What does the district MTSS team need to abandon?

3. What might the district MTSS team need to reconsider or adapt?

These discussions developed into a districtwide continuous feedback loop that included all school sites and collaborative teams. From here, the district MTSS improvement team was able to identify successful, tested ideas from PDSA cycles and adopt them for other schools throughout the district. Over the year, the district and site collaborative teams stayed focused on PDSA cycles that reduced suspension and expulsion rates, especially for students with disabilities.

This case study highlights continuous improvement as a district MTSS improvement team. We emphasize that continuous improvement is woven throughout all the elements of an MTSS framework. The act of continuous improvement is reflected in small PDSA cycles that add up to significant systemwide improvement.

Answer the following questions about the case study and discuss them with your team. See page 128 for a reproducible version of these questions.

- What did you notice or learn from the case study?

- How does the case study exemplify the core components of this chapter?

- How do the team's actions in the case study serve the goal of ensuring all students learn?

Team Activity

The team activity allows you to reflect on what you have read and apply your team's learning. It is an opportunity to assess your organization's current state and decide the best next steps for generating continuous improvement within your MTSS framework. Each member should answer the questions in the team activity individually and then share responses with the team. See page 129 for a reproducible version of this activity.

- What portion of the chapter resonated with you most?

- What is your organization's current reality when it comes to continuous improvement?

- What do you think needs to change in your organization?

- What effective practices do you think need to continue in your organization?

- What steps do you suggest your organization take to enact continuous improvement?

Component Audit

The component audit for continuous improvement guides you to assess the most essential elements to build a strong foundation for the work ahead. After reading this chapter to learn about defining continuous improvement, using PDSA cycles in collaborative teams, and developing effective feedback loops, use the following steps to complete the component audit with your teams.

1. Have team members independently score the implementation status of each of the listed components in your school or district.

2. Compare scores within the team.

3. Discuss with your team to determine which component will be the most effective starting point—which one will have the biggest impact right now?

Figure 6.3 displays the component audit for continuous improvement. See page 130 for a reproducible version of this component audit.

Component	Essential Elements	Status
Continuous Improvement Defined Educators and leaders understand the principles and aims of continuous improvement.	• Leaders and improvement teams establish a focused set of areas to improve across the school or organization. • Leaders and improvement teams determine how to measure the improvement and what data to collect.	☐ Not yet implemented ☐ Partially implemented ☐ Fully implemented ☐ Sustaining implementation
The Plan-Do-Study-Act Cycle for Collaborative Teams Collaborative teams engage in short, iterative improvement cycles.	• Teams try new strategies and analyze their impact on student learning. • Teams make decisions about whether to adopt, adapt, or abandon practices based on data.	☐ Not yet implemented ☐ Partially implemented ☐ Fully implemented ☐ Sustaining implementation
Effective Feedback Loops Schools and districts have a feedback loop process to disseminate new efforts and collect feedback.	• Schools and districts share and try new strategies through site-level and collaborative teams. • School and district improvement teams collect feedback from collaborative teams. • Schools and districts engage in ongoing feedback loops.	☐ Not yet implemented ☐ Partially implemented ☐ Fully implemented ☐ Sustaining implementation

Figure 6.3: MTSS component audit—Continuous improvement.

Action Plan

Based on the results of your team activity and component audit, develop your action plan for implementing continuous improvement, as shown in figure 6.4. A reproducible version appears on page 131. In this sample, the team has selected developing effective feedback loops as their focal component. The action plan they have created will help them connect with their district and improve their implementation status.

Beginning date: _____	**Continuous improvement** **Component:** Developing effective feedback loops (schools and districts have a feedback loop process to disseminate new efforts and collect feedback)	Check when completed
Action plan	Create a process where schools work with the district to share and try new strategies through site-level and collaborative teams. Connect with other school leadership and improvement teams to create a process.	
	Collect feedback from collaborative teams within our school. Ensure collection of concrete information from collaborative teams on a monthly basis.	
	Engage in ongoing feedback loops with the district. Establish a line of communication with the district office on this topic.	
How will you monitor the implementation? What evidence will you examine?	• Create feedback loop process in collaboration with other schools. • Compile agendas and notes of collaborative team meetings and highlight new strategies used during that month. • Document how data are collected and shared around the school on a monthly basis.	

Figure 6.4: Sample action plan for MTSS implementation—Continuous improvement.

Summary

This chapter summarizes the cycle of continuous improvement for an MTSS framework. This process ties the elements of the framework—collaborative leadership, universal access, a continuum of tiered supports, and data-based decision making—together. Just as an MTSS framework uses data to continually respond to student needs, continuous improvement means using data and evidence to constantly improve the system itself. Collaborative teams can use PDSA cycles to efficiently test new instructional strategies and supports. At the school and district levels, MTSS improvement teams can set up effective feedback loops to learn from collaborative teams and spread best practices throughout the organization.

Chapter 6 Case Study Discussion Questions

Answer the following questions about the case study in chapter 6 (page 124) and discuss them with your team.

- What did you notice or learn from the case study?

- How does the case study exemplify the core components of this chapter?

- How do the team's actions in the case study serve the goal of ensuring all students learn?

Chapter 6 Team Activity: Continuous Improvement

The team activity allows you to reflect on what you have read in chapter 6 and apply your team's learning. It is an opportunity to assess your organization's current state and decide the best next steps for generating continuous improvement within your MTSS framework. Each member should answer the questions in the team activity individually and then share responses with the team.

- What portion of the chapter resonated with you most?

- What is your organization's current reality when it comes to continuous improvement?

- What do you think needs to change in your organization?

- What effective practices do you think need to continue in your organization?

- What steps do you suggest your organization take to enact continuous improvement?

Chapter 6 Component Audit: Continuous Improvement

To establish your current status with continuous-improvement concepts and processes, complete the following audit.

1. Have team members independently score the implementation status of each of the identified components in your school or district.

2. Compare scores within the team.

3. Discuss with your team to determine which component will be the most effective starting point—which one will have the biggest impact right now?

Component	Essential Elements	Status
Continuous Improvement Defined Educators and leaders understand the principles and aims of continuous improvement.	• Leaders and improvement teams establish a focused set of areas to improve across the school or organization. • Leaders and improvement teams determine how to measure the improvement and what data to collect.	☐ Not yet implemented ☐ Partially implemented ☐ Fully implemented ☐ Sustaining implementation
The Plan-Do-Study-Act Cycle for Collaborative Teams Collaborative teams engage in short, iterative improvement cycles.	• Teams try new strategies and analyze their impact on student learning. • Teams make decisions about whether to adopt, adapt, or abandon practices based on data.	☐ Not yet implemented ☐ Partially implemented ☐ Fully implemented ☐ Sustaining implementation
Effective Feedback Loops Schools and districts have a feedback loop process to disseminate new efforts and collect feedback.	• Schools and districts share and try new strategies through site-level and collaborative teams. • School and district improvement teams collect feedback from collaborative teams. • Schools and districts engage in ongoing feedback loops.	☐ Not yet implemented ☐ Partially implemented ☐ Fully implemented ☐ Sustaining implementation

Chapter 6 Action Plan for MTSS Implementation:
Continuous Improvement

Based on the results of your team activity and component audit, develop your action plan for implementing continuous improvement. Fill in the component of continuous improvement that you have selected as your focus. Then, list tangible actions that will help improve the status of this component in your school or district, perhaps using the essential elements listed in the component audit as a guide. Finally, define the evidence that you will use to monitor your progress. This action-plan template will build through each chapter into a strategic plan to set the course for long-term implementation.

Beginning date: _____	Continuous improvement Component:	Check when completed
Action plan		
How will you monitor the implementation? What evidence will you examine?		

Epilogue

Toward a Cohesive Approach

In the previous chapters, we shared the essential components of an effective and sustainable MTSS framework: collaborative leadership structures, an inclusive instructional framework that provides all students with high-quality core instruction, a continuum of responses for students who need support or intervention to succeed, and a relentless focus on data. These elements are integrated through cycles of continuous improvement that provide feedback at every level, from the classroom to the district office.

Building an MTSS framework is hard work; it takes time and requires deep collaboration and problem solving. There is no easy way to build a system that supports learning for all, and if you are looking for a quick fix, then MTSS will be challenging to implement. There is no cookie-cutter approach that will work in every situation, which is why this book provides a framework that allows and in fact requires customization for your school or district.

For an initiative like MTSS to work, an organization must have clarity of language and purpose. Be honest about what MTSS is and the potential challenges. The organization must focus on specific outcomes, engage stakeholders in reflective feedback, and stay disciplined about cycles of continuous improvement (Martin, 2012). Leaders of an organization must ensure every stakeholder participates and commits to building, improving, and enhancing MTSS structures to improve outcomes for all students.

For MTSS to be successful and sustainable, it cannot be optional. We bring this to your attention because too many organizations give teams the choice of whether or not to engage with MTSS. Although choice is important to building autonomy, allowing stakeholders to opt out and work against the organization's own mission and goals will result in a state of chaos. Outstanding organizations should focus on building consensus around why MTSS is important and what it means for each member. Clarity is key to organizational strength and the implementation of an MTSS framework that can serve students effectively.

Teams that focus on implementing systems, designing strategies, and reflecting on their learning will build coherence, commitment, and obligation toward the work and goals of the organization.

As you assess your current reality, we offer some final considerations and tools for getting started in your work of building an MTSS framework.

Where to Begin

After completing the component audits, we recommend you select the chapter that best reflects your school or district needs. This allows teams to start where participants can experience the most impact. Consider the following guidance to select your starting point.

- Is there hesitation or resistance to MTSS?

    + If there is hesitation, consider starting with communication and messaging (chapter 2, page 19).

    + If there is resistance, then consider prioritizing which component of the framework (chapters 2–6) is the most urgent for your organization and will generate the most interest among staff.

- Do we know who will lead the work of building a framework?

    + If not, consider MTSS improvement teams (chapter 2, page 19).

- Is there clarity, focus, engagement, and organizational discipline around MTSS?

    + If you lack clarity, start with chapter 2, "Collaborative Leadership" (page 19).

    + If you lack focus, start with chapter 5, "Data-Based Decision Making" (page 93), to prioritize the data you want to improve.

    + If you lack engagement, start with chapter 3, "Universal Access" (page 41).

    + If you lack discipline, start with chapter 6, "Continuous Improvement" (page 117).

- Are there clearly defined goals for implementing MTSS? Do you know what you want to accomplish first?

    + If intentions are unclear, consider chapter 4, "A Continuum of Tiered Supports" (page 59), to deepen understanding of a continuum of tiered supports as a foundation for MTSS.

    + If goals are in place, consider prioritizing which component of the framework (chapters 2–6) is most urgent. While organizations need to address the whole framework, as a starting point it is helpful to consider which actions might have the highest impact.

Team Activity and Action Plan

The final team activity (exemplified in figure E.1) allows you to reflect on the content of this book in its entirety. Each member should answer the questions in the team activity individually and then share responses with the team. The team can synthesize the individual responses to form a picture of where their school or district is with MTSS. See page 138 for a reproducible version of this activity.

MTSS Framework	What about this chapter is a strength for your organization or team?	What about this chapter is an area for improvement for your organization or team?	What about this chapter is an opportunity for your organization or team?	What are one or two actions you suggest your organization or team take in relation to this chapter?
Chapter 2: Collaborative Leadership	We have sent teams to training on professional collaboration.	We need to build in protected time weekly for collaboration.	Since we are just starting out, we have the opportunity to start with an MTSS team.	• Work with leadership to address collaboration time in master schedule. • Send survey to possible MTSS team members to see if they able to join.
Chapter 3: Universal Access	We are revisiting standards to refine our instruction and assessment.	Tier 1 is not as strong as we would like based on the numbers in our Tier 2 and Tier 3.	Learn more about how to create learning experiences with greater access.	• Continue to revisit standards. • Learn more about UDL.
Chapter 4: A Continuum of Tiered Supports	We have interventions in place.	• We don't have clear points for students to enter and exit intervention. • We have only a few options in intervention curriculum, creating a one-size-fits-all approach in some cases.	Determine the number of students moving in and out of intervention.	Look at intervention data for student movement.

Figure E.1: Team activity.

continued →

MTSS Framework	What about this chapter is a strength for your organization or team?	What about this chapter is an area for improvement for your organization or team?	What about this chapter is an opportunity for your organization or team?	What are one or two actions you suggest your organization or team take in relation to this chapter?
Chapter 5: Data-Based Decision Making	We collect a lot of data throughout the year.	We are inconsistent with reviewing data: some data we collect and look at and some we never get to.	Complete an assessment audit.	Create a calendar of our assessments and schedule time to analyze.
Chapter 6: Continuous Improvement for Sustaining MTSS	This is an area of learning for us. Teachers plan together and look at data.	We are limited in this area. We don't really go back and adjust lessons and assessments after we are done with the unit.	Look to see how we can apply continuous-improvement efforts in a challenge area we are currently facing.	Have a team look at a challenge area to see how we can use continuous improvement.

Based on the team activities and the MTSS component audits from each chapter, use the comprehensive action plan to prioritize broad actions for MTSS implementation across your organization. Figure E.2 displays an example of a team that has so far prioritized actions around collaborative leadership. A reproducible version appears on page 139.

We hope the information in this book provides your team and organization with perspectives on how to build an MTSS framework and how to reflect on the development and improvement of your MTSS framework. Ultimately, you and your team *can* build an effective and sustainable framework for your organization! Keep in mind that identifying a starting point is half the battle. Commit to the vision of an MTSS framework, create goals to put that vision into action, execute those goals, revisit the goals and refine continually, and improved student achievement will follow.

MTSS Framework	List the actions each member suggested in the team activity.	Use a consensus process to prioritize those actions in order of impact.	Determine the who, what, when, and how of your top-two actions for building MTSS from the previous column.	Determine a check-in date and completion date for each action.
Chapter 2: Collaborative Leadership	Teacher 1: Could we get coverage during morning prep for PLC time? Principal: Some districts have early release or late starts—is that something we could do? Counselor: How might we use different staffing to provide collaboration time?	1. Staffing and coverage to allow time for collaboration 2. Early release or late start	The teacher and counselor will work to see who might be able to provide coverage. The principal will check with the district office about early release or late start possibilities.	We will meet tomorrow afternoon to make a possible schedule. We will check in at the district meeting next week.
Chapter 3: Universal Access				
Chapter 4: A Continuum of Tiered Supports				
Chapter 5: Data-Based Decision Making				
Chapter 6: Continuous Improvement for Sustaining MTSS				

Figure E.2: Sample comprehensive action plan for MTSS implementation.

Epilogue Team Activity

The final team activity allows you to reflect on the content of this book in its entirety. Each member should answer the questions in the team activity individually and then share responses with the team.

MTSS Framework	What about this chapter is a strength for your organization or team?	What about this chapter is an area for improvement for your organization or team?	What about this chapter is an opportunity for your organization or team?	What are one or two actions you suggest your organization or team take in relation to this chapter?
Chapter 2: Collaborative Leadership				
Chapter 3: Universal Access				
Chapter 4: A Continuum of Tiered Supports				
Chapter 5: Data-Based Decision Making				
Chapter 6: Continuous Improvement for Sustaining MTSS				

Comprehensive Action Plan for MTSS Implementation

Based on the team activities and the MTSS component audits from each chapter, use the action plan to prioritize actions for MTSS implementation across your organization.

MTSS Framework	List the actions each member suggested in the team activity.	Use a consensus process to prioritize those actions in order of impact.	Determine the who, what, when, and how of your top-two actions for building MTSS from the previous column.	Determine a check-in date and completion date for each action.
Chapter 2: Collaborative Leadership				
Chapter 3: Universal Access				
Chapter 4: A Continuum of Tiered Supports				
Chapter 5: Data-Based Decision Making				
Chapter 6: Continuous Improvement for Sustaining MTSS				

References and Resources

Adelman, H., & Taylor, L. (2018). *Transforming student and learning supports: Developing a unified, comprehensive, and equitable system.* San Diego, CA: Cognella Academic Publishing.

Allain, J. K., & Eberhardt, N. C. (2011). *RtI: The forgotten tier—A practical guide for building a data-driven Tier 1 instructional process.* Stockton, KS: Rowe Publishing and Design.

Bailey, T. R. (2019, September 20). *Is MTSS the new RTI? Depends on where you live.* Accessed at https://mtss4success.org/blog/mtss-new-rti-depends-where-you-live on March 1, 2022.

Barber, M., Rodriguez, N., & Artis, E. (2016). *Deliverology in practice: How educational leaders are improving student outcomes.* Thousand Oaks, CA: Corwin Press.

Bernhardt, V. L. (2018). *Data analysis for continuous school improvement* (4th ed.). New York: Routledge.

Bolman, L. G., & Deal, T. E. (2013). *Reframing organizations: Artistry, choice, and leadership* (5th ed.). San Francisco: Jossey-Bass.

Brown-Chidsey, R., & Bickford, R. (2016). *Practical handbook of Multi-Tiered Systems of Support: Building academic and behavioral success in schools.* New York: Guilford Press.

Bryk, A. S. (2020). *Improvement in action: Advancing quality in America's schools.* Cambridge, MA: Harvard Education Press.

Bryk, A. S., Gomez, L. M., Grunow, A., & LeMahieu, P. G. (2015). *Learning to improve: How America's schools can get better at getting better.* Cambridge, MA: Harvard Education Press.

Buffum, A., Mattos, M., & Malone, J. (2018). *Taking action: A handbook for RTI at Work.* Bloomington, IN: Solution Tree Press.

Buffum, A., Mattos, M., & Weber, C. (2009). *Pyramid response to intervention: RTI, professional learning communities, and how to respond when kids don't learn.* Bloomington, IN: Solution Tree Press.

California Department of Education. (2020). *Definition of MTSS.* Accessed at www.cde.ca.gov/ci/cr/ri/mtsscomprti2.asp on November 2, 2021.

CAST. (2018). *The UDL guidelines*. Accessed at http://udlguidelines.cast.org/ on November 7, 2020.

CEEDAR Center. (2017). *High-leverage practices crosswalk*. Accessed at https://ceedar.education.ufl.edu/wp-content/uploads/2017/11/HLP-Crosswalk-with-PSEL1.pdf on November 7, 2021.

Colorado Department of Education. (n.d.). *Colorado Multi-Tiered System of Supports (CO-MTSS)*. Accessed at www.cde.state.co.us/fedprograms/districtwide-comtss on November 2, 2021.

Cook, B. G, Tankersley, M., & Harjusola-Webb, S. (2008). Evidence-based special education and professional wisdom: Putting it all together. *Intervention in School and Clinic, 44*(2), 105–111.

Coyne, P., Evans, M., & Karger, J. (2017). Use of a UDL literacy environment by middle school students with intellectual and developmental disabilities. *Intellectual and Developmental Disabilities, 55*(1), 4–14.

DuFour, R., DuFour, R., Eaker, R., & Many, T. (2006). *Learning by doing: A handbook for Professional Learning Communities at Work* (1st ed.). Bloomington, IN: Solution Tree Press.

DuFour, R., DuFour, R., Eaker, R., Many, T. W., & Mattos, M. (2016). *Learning by doing: A handbook for Professional Learning Communities at Work* (3rd ed.). Bloomington, IN: Solution Tree Press.

DuFour, R., DuFour, R., Eaker, R., Mattos, M., & Muhammad, A. (2021). *Revisiting Professional Learning Communities at Work: Proven insights for sustained, substantive school improvement* (2nd ed.). Bloomington, IN: Solution Tree Press.

Every Student Succeeds Act of 2015, Pub. L. No. 114-95, 20 U.S.C. § 1177 (2015). Accessed at https://www.congress.gov/114/plaws/publ95/PLAW-114publ95.pdf on March 16, 2022.

Florida Department of Education. (n.d.). *Florida Problem Solving/Response to Intervention Project*. Accessed at www.florida-rti.org/floridaMTSS/mtf.htm on November 2, 2021.

Friziellie, H., Schmidt, J. A., & Spiller, J. (2016). *Yes we can! General and special educators collaborating in a professional learning community*. Bloomington, IN: Solution Tree Press.

Gouvernement du Québec. (2016). *Reference framework and guide for schools: Working with students with behavioral difficulties*. Accessed at http://www.education.gouv.qc.ca/fileadmin/site_web/documents/dpse/adaptation_serv_compl/14-00479_cadre_intervention_eleves_difficultes_comportement_EN.pdf on March 1, 2022.

Government of Alberta. (2018, July). *Inclusive education: Conversation guide for the video—Making sense of RTI in the Alberta context*. Accessed at https://www.alberta.ca/assets/documents/ed-video-discussion-guide-9-making-sense-of-rti.pdf on March 1, 2022.

Government of British Columbia. (2022, January 31). *Inclusive education resources.* https:// www2.gov.bc.ca/gov/content/education-training/k-12/teach/resources-for-teachers /inclusive-education on March 1, 2022.

Government of Manitoba. (n.d.). *School attendance.* Accessed at https://www.edu.gov.mb.ca /k12/attendance/educators_info.html on March 1, 2022.

Government of Northwest Territories. (2017, March). *Guidelines for inclusive school-ing: Supporting the NWT Ministerial Directive on Inclusive Schooling.* Accessed at https://www.ece.gov.nt.ca/sites/ece/files/resources/inclusiveschoolingmanualand guidelines-educatorversion-english.pdf on March 1, 2022.

Government of Nova Scotia. (n.d.). *Multi-tiered system of supports (MTSS).* Accessed at https://www.ednet.ns.ca/psp/equity-inclusive-education/multi-tiered-system -supports on February 21, 2022.

Government of Nunavut. (n.d.). *Nunavut K–6 teacher planning guide.* Accessed at https:// governor.hawaii.gov/wp-content/uploads/2016/07/Policy-Nunavut.pdf on March 1, 2022.

Hall, L. L. (2016, April 27). *Plan-do-study-act (PDSA): Accelerate quality improvement in your practice.* Accessed at https://edhub.ama-assn.org/steps-forward/module /2702507 on June 6, 2022.

Hannigan, J. D., & Hannigan, J. E. (2021). *The MTSS start-up guide: Ensuring equity, access, and inclusivity for all students.* Thousand Oaks, CA: Corwin.

Harvard Business Review Analytic Services. (2019). *Overcoming barriers to data impact: New tools and a new data mindset can bring about real-time decision making* [Briefing paper]. Accessed at www.splunk.com/pdfs/analyst-reports/overcoming-barriers -to-data-impact.pdf on April 26, 2021.

Hattie, J. (2015, June). *What works best in education: The politics of collaborative expertise.* London: Pearson. Accessed at https://www.pearson.com/content/dam/corporate /global/pearson-dot-com/files/hattie/150526_ExpertiseWEB_V1.pdf on March 8, 2022.

Higher Education Opportunity Act of 2008, Pub. L. No. 110–315, 122 U.S.C. § 3078 (2008). Accessed at https://www.govinfo.gov/content/pkg/PLAW-110publ315/pdf /PLAW-110publ315.pdf on March 16, 2022.

Howard, K. L. (2006). Teacher perspectives: UDL in the elementary classroom. In D. H. Rose & A. Meyer (Eds.), *A practical reader in Universal Design for Learning* (pp. 49–56). Cambridge, MA: Harvard Education Press.

Hughes, C., & Dexter, D. D. (n.d.). The use of RTI to identify students with learning disabilities: A review of the research. *RTI Action Network.* Accessed at http://www .rtinetwork.org/learn/research/use-rti-identify-students-learning-disabilities -review-research on February 23, 2022.

Illinois MTSS Network. (n.d.). *Illinois MTSS network at a glance.* Accessed at https://ilmtss .net/about-us/multi-tiered-system-of-supports-mtss on November 2, 2021.

Individuals with Disabilities Education Act of 2004, 20 U.S.C. § 1400–1401 (2020).

Institute for Healthcare Improvement. (n.d.). *Science of improvement: Linking tests of change.* Accessed at www.ihi.org/resources/Pages/HowtoImprove/Scienceof ImprovementLinkingTestsofChange.aspx on November 2, 2021.

Institute for Healthcare Improvement. (2003). *The Breakthrough Series: IHI's collaborative model for achieving breakthrough improvement.* Accessed at www.ihi.org/resources /Pages/IHIWhitePapers/TheBreakthroughSeriesIHIsCollaborativeModel forAchievingBreakthroughImprovements.aspx on May 19, 2021.

Institute of Education Sciences. (n.d.). *The What Works Clearinghouse.* Accessed at https:// ies.ed.gov/ncee/wwc/ on March 30, 2021.

Kamphaus, R. W., & Reynolds, C. R. (2015). *BASC-3 behavioral and emotional screening system.* Bloomington, MN: Pearson Clinical Assessment.

Kansas State Department of Education. (2019). *Kansas State Department of Education: Kansas Multi-Tier System of Supports and alignment fact sheet 2019.* Accessed at www.ksde.org/Portals/0/ECSETS/FactSheets/FactSheet-MTSS.pdf on November 2, 2021.

Langley, G. J., Moen, R. D., Nolan, K. M., Nolan, T. W. Norman, C. L., & Provost, L. P. (2009). *The improvement guide: A practical approach to enhancing organizational performance* (2nd ed.). San Francisco: Jossey-Bass.

Maier, M. P., Pate, J. L., Gibson, N. M., Hilgert, L., Hull, K., & Campbell, P. C. (2016). A quantitative examination of school leadership and response to intervention. *Learning Disabilities Research and Practice, 31*(2), 103–112.

Mandinach, E. B., & Gummer, E. (Eds.). (2019). *Data for continuous programmatic improvement: Steps colleges of education must take to become a data culture.* New York: Routledge.

Martin, K. (2012). *The outstanding organization: Generate business results by eliminating chaos and building the foundation for everyday excellence.* New York: McGraw-Hill.

Massachusetts Department of Elementary and Secondary Education. (n.d.). *Multi-Tiered System of Support: Blueprint for MA.* Accessed at www.doe.mass.edu/sfss/mtss /blueprint.pdf on November 2, 2021.

McCart, A., & Miller, D. (2020). *Leading equity-based MTSS for all students.* Thousand Oaks, CA: Corwin Press.

McCray, E. D., Kamman, M., Brownell, M. T., & Robinson, S. (2017). *High-leverage practices and evidence-based practices: A promising pair.* Gainesville, FL: CEEDAR Center. Accessed at https://ceedar.education.ufl.edu/wp-content/uploads/2017/12 /HLPs-and-EBPs-A-Promising-Pair.pdf on March 20, 2021.

McIntosh, K., & Goodman, S. (2016). *Integrated Multi-Tiered Systems of Support: Blending RTI and PBIS*. New York: Guilford Press.

McLeskey, J., Barringer, M-D., Billingsley, B., Brownwell, M., Jackson, D., Kennedy, M., et al. (2017, January). *High-leverage practices in special education*. Arlington, VA: Council for Exceptional Children & CEEDAR Center.

Mercado, F. (2018). Whole child framework: Supporting educators in their plight toward MTSS and equity. *Journal for Leadership, Equity, and Research, 4*(2), 1–14.

Metcalf, T. (2015a). *What's your plan? Accurate decision making within a Multi-Tier System of Supports: Critical areas in Tier 1*. Accessed at www.rtinetwork.org/essential/tiered instruction/tier1/accurate-decision-making-within-a-multi-tier-system-of-supports-critical-areas-in-tier-1 on November 2, 2021.

Metcalf, T. (2015b). *What's your plan? Accurate decision making within a Multi-Tier System of Supports: Critical areas in Tier 2*. Accessed at www.rtinetwork.org/essential/tiered instruction/tier2/whats-your-plan-accurate-decision-making-within-a-multi-tier-system-of-supports-critical-areas-in-tier-2 on November 2, 2021.

Meyer, A., Rose, D. H., & Gordon, D. (2014). *Universal design for learning: Theory and practice*. Wakefield, MA: CAST.

Michigan Department of Education. (n.d.). *MiMTSS: Michigan's Multi-Tiered System of Supports*. Accessed at www.michigan.gov/mde/Services/school-performance-supports/mtss on November 2, 2021.

Moore, R., & Croft, M. (2018). *Reducing barriers to educator data use*. Accessed at https://www.act.org/content/dam/act/unsecured/documents/R1662-data-use-barriers-2018-01.pdf on February 28, 2022.

Muhammad, A., & Cruz, L. F. (2019). *Time for change: Four essential skills for transformational school and district leaders*. Bloomington, IN: Solution Tree Press.

Navarro, S., Zervas, P., Gesa, R., & Sampson, D. (2016). Developing teachers' competences for designing inclusive learning experiences. *Educational Technology & Society, 19*(1), 17–27.

Nelson, L. L., & Basham, J. D. (2014). *A blueprint for UDL: Considering the design of implementation*. Lawrence, KS: Universal Design for Learning Implementation and Research Network.

New Brunswick Department of Education and Early Childhood Development. (2015, November). *Guidelines and standards: Educational planning for students with diverse learning needs*. Accessed at https://www2.gnb.ca/content/dam/gnb/Departments/ed/pdf/K12/curric/Resource/GuidelinesStandardsEducationalPlanningStudentsWith Exceptionalities.pdf on March 1, 2022.

Newfoundland and Labrador Department of Education. (2020, October). *Responsive teaching and learning policy*. Accessed at https://www.gov.nl.ca/education/files/RTL-Policy.pdf on March 1, 2022.

New York State Education Department. (n.d.). *Information for educators and schools.* Accessed at http://www.nysed.gov/essa/information-educators-and-schools on November 2, 2021.

Novak, K., & Rodriguez, K. (2016). *Universally designed leadership: Applying UDL to systems and schools.* Wakefield, MA: CAST.

Office of Educational Technology. (2017, January). *Reimagining the role of technology in education: 2017 National Education Technology Plan update.* Washington, DC: Author. Accessed at https://tech.ed.gov/files/2017/01/NETP17.pdf on November 2, 2021.

Ontario Human Rights Commission. (2018, March). *Policy: Accessible education for students with disabilities.* Accessed at https://www.ohrc.on.ca/sites/default/files/Policy%20on%20accessible%20education%20for%20students%20with%20disabilities_FINAL_EN.pdf on March 1, 2022.

Ontario Ministry of Education. (2013). *Learning for all: A guide to effective assessment and instruction for all students, kindergarten to grade 12.* Accessed at https://files.ontario.ca/edu-learning-for-all-2013-en-2022-01-28.pdf on March 1, 2022.

Oregon Department of Education. (n.d.). *Multi-Tiered System of Supports* (*MTSS*). Accessed at www.oregon.gov/ode/students-and-family/GraduationImprovement/Documents/MTSS.pdf on November 2, 2021.

Rao, K., Smith, S. J., & Lowrey, K. A. (2017). UDL and intellectual disability: What do we know and where do we go? *Intellectual and Developmental Disabilities, 55*(1), 37–47.

Reeves, D. (2021). *Deep change leadership: A model for renewing and strengthening schools and districts.* Bloomington, IN: Solution Tree Press.

Rodriguez, B. J., Loman, S. L., & Borgmeier, C. (2016). Tier 2 interventions in positive behavior support: A survey of school implementation. *Preventing School Failure, 60*(2), 94–105.

Rogers, P., Smith, W. R., Buffum, A., & Mattos, M. (2020). *Best practices at Tier 3: Intensive interventions for remediation, elementary.* Bloomington, IN: Solution Tree Press.

Rose, D. H., & Meyer, A. (2006). *A practical reader in Universal Design for Learning.* Cambridge, MA: Harvard Education Press.

Rose, T. (2016). *The end of average: How we succeed in a world that values sameness.* New York: HarperOne.

Sailor, W. (2015). Advances in schoolwide inclusive school reform. *Remedial and Special Education, 36*(2), 94–99.

Sailor, W. (2017). Equity as a basis for inclusive educational systems change. *Australasian Journal of Special Education, 41*(1), 1–17.

Sailor, W., & McCart, A. B. (2014). Stars in alignment. *Research and Practice for Persons With Severe Disabilities, 39*(1), 55–64.

Saskatchewan Ministry of Education. (2020). *Framework for a provincial education plan 2020–2030*. Accessed at https://pubsaskdev.blob.core.windows.net/pubsask -prod/114715/2019%252BPEP%252BFramework%252BENG%252BApr2021 %252BFinal.pdf on March 1, 2022.

Senge, P. M. (1990). *The fifth discipline: The art and practice of the learning organization* (1st ed.). New York: Doubleday.

Shafritz, J. M., Ott, J. S., & Jang, Y. S. (2016). *Classics of organization theory* (8th ed.). Boston: Cengage Learning.

Smith, A. (2014, April 23–24). *Stuart leadership meeting workshop 5* [Conference presentation]. Stuart Foundation California Leaders in Education (SCALE), Los Angeles, CA.

Tennessee Department of Education. (2018, March). *Overview of student supports in Tennessee*. Accessed at www.tn.gov/content/dam/tn/education/reports/student_supports_ overview.pdf on November 2, 2021.

UDL on Campus. (n.d.). *About UDL*. Accessed at http://udloncampus.cast.org/page/udl _about on November 2, 2021.

U.S. Department of Education. (2017, October 2). *Early learning: Early literacy initiative resources*. Accessed at https://www2.ed.gov/about/inits/ed/earlylearning/early-literacy /elit-resources.html on April 1, 2022.

Wayman, J. C., Midgley, S., & Stringfield, S. (2006). *Leadership for data-based decision making: Collaborative educator teams*. Paper presented at the Annual Meeting of the American Educational Research Association, San Francisco.

Whitley, J., & Hollweck, T. (2020, September 9). Inclusion and equity in education: Current policy reform in Nova Scotia, Canada. *Prospects, 49*, 297–312.

Williams, A. (2020). *Teachers' perspectives on implementing universal design for learning* (Publication No. 28031523) [Doctoral dissertation, California State University, Fresno]. ProQuest.

Wolfram, P., & Peine, H. (2020, March). *Planning for success post COVID-19* [Webinar]. Council of Administrators of Special Education and the Council for Exceptional Children.

Yee, N. (2020). *Review of inclusive and special education: Interim update*. Accessed at https:// yukon.ca/sites/yukon.ca/files/edu/review-inclusive-special-education-interim -update_1.pdf on March 1, 2022.

Zajic, D. [@hdzajic]. (2019, May 29). *"Supports are tiered, NOT the students" -Rebecca Zumeta Edmonds on supporting children with a multi-tier system of support. A child requires a full continuum of intensity calibrated to their weaknesses AND strengths.* [Tweet]. Twitter. Accessed at https://twitter.com/hdzajic/status/1133721666704609282 on November 5, 2021.

Index

W

Collective Efficacy in a PLC at Work®
Matt Navo and Jared J. Savage
How did one of California's lowest-performing districts become a top turnaround district? It all came down to building collective team efficacy. Dive into this resource to find parallels to your own story and apply the lessons learned at Sanger Unified to the school community you serve.
BKF973

The Wraparound Guide
Leigh Colburn and Linda Beggs
Your school has the power to help students overcome barriers to well-being and achievement—from mental health issues to substance abuse to trauma. With this timely guide, discover actionable steps for launching and sustaining wraparound services embedded within your school that support the whole child.
BKF956

Educator's Guide to Schoolwide Positive Behavioral Interventions and Supports
Jason E. Harlacher and Billie Jo Rodriguez
Discover how to create an encouraging, productive school culture using the Schoolwide Positive Behavioral Interventions and Supports (SWPBIS) framework. This title includes the authors' personal experiences in applying SWPBIS and explores practical examples of what the elements and tiers of this model look like in practice.
BKL030

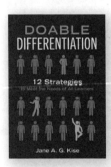

Doable Differentiation
Jane A.G. Kise
Differentiating for students' learning preferences can often seem too complex and complicated for too little gain. With *Doable Differentiation*, you will discover a series of straightforward, high-reward strategies that educators like you use daily to support, engage, and challenge students with diverse learning styles.
BKF952

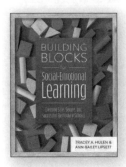

Building Blocks for Social-Emotional Learning
Tracey A. Hulen and Ann-Bailey Lipsett
Support the growth of your students with meaningful, effective social-emotional learning. You'll engage in deep reflection and discover ways to refine instruction, lesson planning, and assessment; promote whole-child development; and foster a productive learning environment for all.
BKG019

Wait! Your professional development journey doesn't have to end with the last pages of this book.

We realize improving student learning doesn't happen overnight. And your school or district shouldn't be left to puzzle out all the details of this process alone.

No matter where you are on the journey, we're committed to helping you get to the next stage.

Take advantage of everything from **custom workshops** to **keynote presentations** and **interactive web and video conferencing**. We can even help you develop an action plan tailored to fit your specific needs.

Let's get the conversation started.

Call 888.763.9045 today.

SolutionTree.com